# THE LONGEST MONDAY

Don Clair

authorHOUSE®

*AuthorHouse*™
*1663 Liberty Drive, Suite 200*
*Bloomington, IN 47403*
*www.authorhouse.com*
*Phone: 1-800-839-8640*

© *2008 Don Clair. All rights reserved.*

*No part of this book may be reproduced, stored in a retrieval system, or transmitted by any means without the written permission of the author.*

*First published by AuthorHouse 1/29/2008*

*ISBN: 978-1-4343-6353-4 (sc)*

*Printed in the United States of America*
*Bloomington, Indiana*

*This book is printed on acid-free paper.*

The Longest Monday by Don Clair

Dear Readers,

The characters in this book are fictional. They represent the generation that experienced the war in Vietnam. I began to tell this story thirty years ago, right after the U.S. Forces failed to free the POWs held by North Vietnam. Having participated in that doomed mission, I carried with me a sense of guilt until I had the opportunity to talk with one of the POWs. I explained to him how sorry I was for letting them down and failing in our attempt to rescue. This POW responded with words of wisdom, "We knew you tried to rescue us, and that meant we weren't forgotten. Your efforts made us stronger."

The vast majority of young men who experienced the Vietnam War didn't come home and turn into dreadful killing machines, or into street bums. Many Vietnam veterans became stronger because of their experiences overseas. The veterans I know returned to the states and became bankers, lawyers, doctors, police officers, and blue- and white-collar workers. They have sought to make the world a better place in which to live, a place where possibilities and dreams can be fulfilled.

The Vietnam experience has shaped my life. Without it, I believe I wouldn't have achieved my goals today. I now do seminars, helping others to realize how our difficult experiences can become catalysts for great personal growth and success.

I became passionate about telling this story when I realized

America never knew how the U.S. Armed Forces did try to rescue our POWs. The events of Kent State and on college campuses across America collided with this effort and naturally received the media's attention. An unpopular war a half-world away with yet another failed attempt to achieve anything must have seemed unimportant at the time. I can't help but question which direction America would have taken if they'd really understood those efforts to rescue our own. Perhaps the tide of public sentiment may have shifted toward those who'd served. Now we'll never know.

My heartfelt dream is for each reader to come away from this book with a better understanding of the sacrifice that was made. The veterans of the Vietnam War were simply young men and women just like you. They were trained for a few weeks and thrown into a world almost impossible to understand.

I want to thank Dr. Rodger Moler, a medic in Nam. Our families are very close friends today. We share life's gifts and challenges. I would like to thank Linda Cope. Without Linda's love for this project and her driving force, this story would still be untold. To the veterans of America, I want to thank you for allowing me to experience freedom.
Sincerely,
Donald Clair

# PROLOGUE

Small hotel on old Route 66, January 3, 2006

> "In life for a story to be fully heard, one has to reach the end before the beginning can mean anything. You must experience the end before you can begin the journey. That is the secret to hearing it all and knowing the ending is the beginning to today's problems."
>
> —Chap Stone

###

Holding tightly on to the sink until his oversized, fat fingers turned nearly blue, his hands were dripping with water that smelled like old chlorine from a swimming pool. It burned in the folds of fat between his multiple chins. He concentrated hard on the water, on the sound the water made as it drained away. He could not help but think this was just like his life. Swirling out of control, spilling down a drain with nothing but a hint of his personal scum left behind.

He wasn't in Vietnam . . . Or Kent, Ohio. He was in a motel on Rt. 66, in Illinois. The fire-hazard, frayed cord of his dreams seemed so clearly cut in two by cheap lamps or the Formica floor peeling away from the trim against the wall.

A broken movie camera played the moment he tried to sleep. It felt like a band of monkeys beating behind his eyes. All he could think of was, Is this really real? The flower, the rose. Thank God he'd sent it before coming south.

He'd paid cash to the florist, like always. Untraceable. Every year from a different city. Always yellow. It would arrive tomorrow on her birthday.

That was something to hold on to if only for a moment, a reason not to pull the trigger one more day.

Soon. He'd make up for all the running, hiding, living in the shadows, end the movie, give into the pain and move into redemption, the only way out. The pills. And now nothing could stop him. Soon. One last mission.

# NEOSHO, MISSOURI, 1968
# CHAP STONE
# CHAPTER 1

> "If you wait, I mean really wait and don't move, you'll get your kill."
>
> —Chap Stone

On a warm spring day, Chap Stone stretched his six-foot-one-inch, lean frame belly down on the cool ground. He'd saved for two years to buy the Seiko 222 pressed against his cheek. The Seiko was a target gun, bull barrel, with a solid walnut stock, smooth as still water. It had intricate carvings on the trim, and its bold action was the finest made in 1968.

Chap's dad had no idea how much the gun had cost, but that was okay. He'd paid for it with his own money, and he was the one who wanted to make the kill this day, not his dad.

Chap had been lying atop the glade for three hours, quiet as a felled tree. He watched the groundhog hole almost four hundred meters away. Every now and then the critter stuck its nose out, but never long enough for Chap to make the kill.

Others would have left, decided it was just a lousy groundhog, not worth the wait. But Chap had a "me against him" philosophy.

That's what made him one of the best hunters in these parts. That, and the way he saw things. Animals always stood out for Chap, and any movement was like a flag running up a pole. Camouflage blinked like a sign crying, "Come and get me!"

But still, the special sight wouldn't have mattered without the patient determination to stay put.

As if proving Chap's point, the groundhog came out of its hole and froze. It started to stand, but before it had a chance, before the Seiko cracked the air, the animal lay dead.

Chap's face split into a grin that put the welcome mat out. He'd nailed that critter's ass. Jiminy Christmas, what a sweet gun. He'd get his deer next fall. This Seiko was the gun of a lifetime.

Chap picked up the little bipod he'd made for the rifle. He walked down the hill, counting off the steps, three hundred and twenty-four meters. He retrieved the groundhog, and saw he'd nailed it on the chin. Not bad. He figured he'd hit a dime and was satisfied.

Folks in Tulane County, Missouri, knew Chap Stone had the strongest pair of hands. What they didn't know was how he punched feed sacks in the barn, and dreamed of entering the ring. He'd grown up milking cows and bucking bales of hay. Now, at the end of his senior year, Chap could throw an eighty-pound bale like it was a giant marshmallow, and he'd never lifted weights in his life.

He hung the groundhog on the fence to join the others he'd

killed this spring. They were destroying the alfalfa fields, and he couldn't let that happen.

An evening's work waited at the milk barns. Chap whistled as he crossed the field. Tonight was his high school graduation, and he saw the rest of his life through a rainbow of freedom.

In the milking parlor, Chap turned the radio to the rock and roll station. He set the volume high, as the hired man, Carl, drove in the first cow. Satisfaction seemed as much a part of Chap's chest as heart and lungs. He fit the milkers to the udder and sang with the radio. After tonight, he was free. He'd go to college, or travel, or do anything that took him away from Neosho.

When he finished milking, Chap washed up. On his way to the house, he rubbed his sleeve against the cool, green shine of his prize possession—a '57 Chevy.

The Chevy had a powerglide transmission. He'd wanted a fourspeed, but the powerglide was all they had.

He didn't care because it was his. Bought it for three hundred and fifty dollars. The outside looked new, and the inside was better than new because Chap fixed it up himself.

Good smells came through the wooden screen door. Mom stood at the sink, chopping an onion for stew. She looked up and smiled as he entered. "I tell you, Chap, you get more handsome every day. Someday you'll kill those girls."

Chap kissed her cheek. She smelled like coffee and bleach. "Where's Dad?"

Mom rolled her eyes. "Where else? He's workin' overtime at the plant."

"He puts in too many hours," Chap said.

"Well, with four children, man takes what he can get, and he's grateful."

Mom was pure English. Dad favored his Choctaw mother, had her hooked nose and high cheekbones. Mom was tender—silk. Dad abrasive—sandpaper. Mom encouraged. Dad controlled. Mom believed in Chap. Dad worried his oldest son would end up a loser, and held it over his head like a tomahawk every time Chap made a mistake.

"You've got a letter, Son," Mom said.

"A letter for me? I never get letters."

"You got a letter today."

Chap knew where it would be. He went in the dim living room and checked the top of the old piano. Wedged between a picture of his sister and the metronome was a white envelope. It was addressed to him. The lefthand corner read "Selective Service."

"I've already registered," he called to his mom as he tore open the envelope.

Mom stood in the doorway. He smelled the onions on her

hands.

"What's the matter, Son? You've gone pale as milk."

Chap didn't answer. He looked at her, then back at the paper.

"What's the matter, Chap?" She drew close enough to flick him with the dishtowel.

"Mom, tell me what this means."

She took hold of one top corner, while Chap held the other. Mom read aloud, "Greetings and salutations from the President of the United States and your community. You have been selected to represent your community in the Armed Forces of the United States. You are hereby ordered to report to the armed AP station in Kansas City, Missouri, for a physical, June 2, 1968. You'll be returned home shortly thereafter."

"What does it mean, Mom?" Chap and his mom looked at the letter for a long time.

"Well, it means you've got to go up there and get a physical," she finally said.

"But I'm only getting out of high school today on the 28th. There's only five days in between. Don't they ever give a guy a break?"

"You're just going up to get a physical, Honey, to see if you're all right. They ain't drafted you. It says you can return home, see?"

Chap wanted to believe her. She was right about most things. "Yeah, I guess that's what it's saying." A bus ticket was tucked in the letter. It wasn't that far to Kansas City. Besides, Chap didn't want anything to ruin tonight's graduation. He could look at this army business like a little vacation.

Mom pulled at his blond tail of hair. "I wish you'd have gotten a haircut, Chap. That ponytail upsets your father."

"It don't matter, Mom. Hey, I'm fourth in my class, and I worked a full-time job, too. I got my whole life ahead of me, and after tonight, I'm free."

Mom chuckled as they hugged. "I love you, Chap." Then more softly, "I'm so proud."

### 

Forty-seven kids graduated in Chap's class, the largest group in the school's history. Some of the kids were going out drinking to celebrate. Chap had to milk at 4:00 a.m. No time to party for a working man.

Four days later, Chap's mom fussed over him at the bus station. She warned him to be careful, and then asked him for the third time if he had his money. He did, and, "Mom, I'm only going to Kansas City." How would she take it when he lit out to see the world?

The bus trip didn't take long. Chap looked with dismay at the tall city buildings, and the traffic. He couldn't get over the black people, they were everywhere. He'd never even met a black person before.

At the hotel, the whole place was full of new recruits and guys like Chap reporting for physicals.

Chap put himself where he could watch all the hubbub. A seat at one of the tables in the hotel bar seemed like a good spot, even if he couldn't drink.

There were guys everywhere, all talking at once, some looking as confused as he probably did, some cocksure and wide-eyed with excitement. There were guys who wanted in the Army, and guys who wanted no part of it. Chap laughed when he overheard two fellas planning to wear girls' underwear so they'd be sure and get rejected. Why would anyone go to those lengths? How could the Army give a crap whose underwear you wore?

This was turning into a real adventure. He'd get to sleep in the hotel tonight, then get the physical over with in the morning, and watch more of the sights as he headed home. Wouldn't be any time; he'd be making plans for a free-rolling summer.

At five-thirty the next morning, Chap was awakened by a horrendous pounding and a voice like God's on judgment day. "Get your ass up!"

He lifted his head from the bunched pillow and tried to focus on the door.

"Rock and roll guys. Rock and roll," the full-throttled voice called.

Chap let his head drop. Some vacation. This was as bad as home. Grumbling, he got dressed and went downstairs to eat breakfast.

Men in white caps and short-sleeved white shirts served bowls of thick white paste. When a military honcho walked by at a slow, leg-swinging pace, Chap complained, "You call this oatmeal, Sir?"

"Take it or leave it, son. Take it or leave it."

He'd leave it. At least the waiter was making the rounds with coffee. Like the other boys, Chap upended his thick china mug as the waiter approached with a pot.

The Kansas City coffee pours like sorghum.

Chap lifted the cup to his lips and sipped just enough to make a mud puddle on his tongue. "This stuff'll kill you," he told the kid across the table. I don't need this garbage in my stomach, he thought.

They walked the two blocks to the AP station. Inside was the most huge gymnasium Chap had ever seen. He figured it could hold two, three thousand people.

Hundreds of young men filled the place, all sizes, all colors, some dressed, some in their underwear. Lord, this Army doesn't leave a guy any pride at all, Chap thought.

Over the resonating blend of voices, Chap heard one sentence again and again, rising clear to the high-domed ceiling, "Here's a number; hang your clothes. Here's a number; hang your clothes."

They handed Chap a number. He found his peg and hung his clothes. It was embarrassing to stand in his jockey shorts. He noticed some guys wearing boxers, others wearing girls' silk panties stretching over their privates. Hair whorled around one guy's navel and arrowed behind the lacy, elastic pink band. Chap had never seen the like. He laughed hard and knew his face flushed red.

"Get in line. Get in line."

Everywhere he looked, Chap saw legs—some bowed, some straight, some brown, some white, skinny or muscular, and all pathetically bare. He took his turn on the platform. The doctors poked and prodded, took x-rays . . . and blood.

It wasn't so bad. At least they were going through it together. As he joined a line of twenty-five boys, Chap relaxed somewhat. Then he saw the three women doctors waiting to do the next part of the exam. His throat felt dry, and he swallowed hard enough to dislodge his Adam's apple. He didn't even know a lady could be a doctor.

"Drop your drawers," one of the ladies called.

*She has to be kidding!*

But, up and down the line guys were skimming their shorts down to their ankles. Chap took a quick look at the ceiling, bent to follow suit, and he was suddenly more naked than he'd ever been in his life.

*What if I get a hard-on, right in front of . . . Oh.*

The doctor smacked Chap right where it hurt.

The black guy next to Chap strangled on laughter. "You cool, ponytail. You cool."

"Cough son, cough," the lady ordered.

Chap couldn't. Sound wouldn't squeeze past the gorge in his throat. The guy beside him nearly doubled over.

"Cough, son, cough." She reached between Chap's legs, and he turned his head so he wouldn't choke in her face.

Apparently, the Army judged Chap's privates intact. He grabbed the elastic to his shorts, yanked them in place and walked weak-kneed down the line. He could still feel the lady doctor's rubber fingers tingling on his nuts.

The next exam was the eyes. The man in the white coat directed Chap to sit. "Tell me the letters on the screen."

Chap put his head in the visor. "This is a trick. There ain't no letters."

"Look at the screen again, son."

"No letters. They're dots. Just dots," Chap said.

"Step over here."

With a tiny dagger of light, the optometrist examined Chap's eyes. "Take a look here. Look at this chart."

The doctor turned the lights on. Chap read the numbers he could see.

The optometrist looked at Chap closely. "Damn, boy. You're color blind."

"I'm not color blind."

"Tell me what color my coat is."

"It's white."

"That's right. Tell me what color this is here." The doctor pointed to a metal lampshade.

"Dark."

"No, what color is this, son?"

"It's dark, Sir."

Chap was pulled out of line and made to look at more pictures, special ones just for him. Another doctor came over and had Chap answer questions about what he saw.

What I have to do this for? This ain't any physical, he thought.

Out of his range of hearing, the two doctors conferred. He couldn't believe all the fuss. He saw better than anybody in Tulane County.

Finally, they said Chap was done. "Get dressed."

He felt more like himself, fully clothed. Back in the gym, they were told to line up in rows of twenty-five.

Each boy was given a number—one, two or three. In the front of the auditorium, an officer screamed for all number ones to step forward and line up against the wall. Boys ambled forth to take their places. Some leaned, some crooked a knee and rested a foot against the tile. A couple slid to their haunches and waited.

"Congratulations," the officer bellowed, pacing along the line, "you have been selected to represent your country in the United States Marine Corp."

The boys stared. Several pulled away from the wall, and stood straighter, their arms hanging at their sides. Others applauded themselves.

"If you do not honorably want to serve in the United States Marines, you do have some options. You may enlist in the Air Force for four years, the Army for three years, or the United States Navy for three years. Those of you who wish to do that may step over there to the Army recruiting board and they will talk to you . . . now." The officer pointed across the gym to the tables where recruiters waited.

Chap sucked air. What a choice! Those poor guys, he thought.

The sergeant turned around and hollered, "Twos, step forward, against the wall."

Chap was a three. He wondered what was coming up for him.

The sergeant walked along the line of guys against the wall, and in the same loud voice said, "Congratulations, it has been decided you will return to your homes and await further notification for service in the United States Armed Forces. Go back to the hotel, get your luggage, and you will be able to catch your bus at zero six hundred hours."

Smiles broke out all along the line as the boys quickly left the gym.

The sergeant clicked his heels briskly, and walked back to where the threes stood, pawn-like, at irregular spaces. He stood before them, starch in his spine and in a voice as distinctive as a doomsday bugle, he yelled, "Congratulations gentlemen. You have just been selected to represent your community in the armed forces with the U. S. Army."

Adventure had become unreality for Chap. He knew he was awake, not dreaming, but this had to be a mistake. He thought of his mom, and even his dad. But they weren't here.

"I'm goin' home," Chap whispered to himself. "I'm gonna travel."

"Gentlemen," the bugle called, "please form a line. We will be marching onto the stage."

Chap had drawn the line. Now, he was just hanging out, waiting for this to be over, so he could go home. Feeling some comfort in his resolution, he followed the stamping feet of the others.

On stage, a little old man stood in a far, dark corner. The arms of his jacket were covered with stripes. Stars and clusters of tiny gold leaves decorated his coat. This might be someone Chap could reason with. He approached the old man and stood beside him.

The sergeant hollered, "Attention."

Chap stood straight like the old guy did. A kid wearing a band uniform came from behind the stage.

"Gentlemen," the sergeant called, "please stand at attention as the lieutenant gives you the oath of the Army of the United States."

"Attention," the little lieutenant called in a thin voice.

Everyone straightened, but Chap. He wasn't having anything to do with this.

"Please raise your right arm as I give you the oath of enlistment," the childish lieutenant continued.

Chap crossed his arms, and legs. He wasn't getting involved.

The lieutenant gave the oath of enlistment. "Congratulations. You are now members of the United States Armed Forces. You'll be loaded on the buses and will be taken to Fort Leonard Wood. Immediately."

The boys started to file out a side door.

"Not me." Chap looked at the kindly old man. "Hey, Pop."

"Yes?" the officer answered in a cold voice.

Chap knew something was different about this man, but he was too angry to care. "Pop, I didn't hold my hand up. I didn't repeat that crap the lieutenant said. I ain't in your damn Army. I'm going home."

Chap felt the back of his head connect with the wall. His feet were off the ground. Close to his face the little old man whispered, "Listen, son. In this whole world, there ain't but two sons of bitches know you never took the oath. And I ain't tellin' a damn soul."

Before Chap could move, the old man hit him once in the side of his neck. Chap wanted to move, but pain paralyzed him.

"MP," the officer called.

"Yes Sir, Sergeant Major," the MP said.

Chap's hands were pulled behind his back. He felt the hard bite of cuffs around his wrists. He managed to drag his gaze to the man who'd inflicted the pain. "I ain't done nothin' to you, man."

The sergeant major stepped close. "Son, you will be in the United States Army. Where are you from?"

"Neosho, Missouri."

The sergeant major addressed the MP. "Please escort this individual to another recruiting station."

The MP took an iron grip on Chap's arm and ushered him out the door.

"Where am I going? My Mom thinks I'll be home on Wednesday. Can't you take these cuffs off me? I ain't gonna hurt you."

The MP didn't respond.

They waited inside a jeep with a closed top. In a few minutes, the lieutenant brought out an envelope and whispered to the MP. Chap overheard the word, "airport."

"Where are we going?" Chap asked as the jeep moved into traffic.

The MP kept his gaze straight ahead.

"Where are we going?"

It was as if Chap hadn't spoken. He leaned a shoulder against the hard seat. The buildings and hubbub of the city he'd gawked at just yesterday looked different now, sinister, like he'd been taken to an evil place. His stomach clenched, his neck still throbbed, and his arms were pulled back at a miserable angle.

After twenty minutes of fighting panic, Chap noticed signs for the airport. He'd never been on a plane. Surely they weren't going to put him on one now. Planes were narrow little tin cans that defied reason, floated on air and took you a million miles from home.

The jeep pulled near a terminal. The MP exited, rounded to Chap's door, and grabbed his arm.

"Don't I have some rights?" Chap asked as he got on his feet.

"Follow me, son."

Chap pulled his arm free. "I ain't your son."

"Right. Follow me, soldier." The MP grabbed Chap's arm again, his grip more bruising than before.

They hurried to the gate for military air flights.

"Where we going?" Chap followed the MP's lead and looked at a screen listing flights.

Atlanta? God, they can't be shipping me to Atlanta, can they?

"You guys told me the recruiting station is in Fort Leonard Wood, Missouri. That's where I'm from. I don't want to go to Atlanta."

The MP pulled Chap forward, all the way to the twin-engine prop run by TWA.

The plane ride lasted an eternity. A bus waited at the Atlanta airport. It had cage wire inside the glass windows, a prison bus. Chap and the MP were the only two passengers who spoke English.

Three hours later they arrived at Fort Gordon, Georgia. It could have been Siberia as far as Chap was concerned. Finally, they took his cuffs off.

"You're gonna stay here, in the barracks like a soldier, or you can go to the guardhouse. What's it gonna be, Stone?" the MP asked him.

Chap rubbed the red gullies on his wrists. "Guess I'll be staying."

### 

Whistles and screams awoke Chap the next morning. "Get up, get up, get your ass up . . . now!"

He had slept in a bay with about sixty other guys. The fast staccato sounds of a foreign tongue came to life, heightening Chap's sense of abduction and isolation.

I'm in trouble. Deep, deep shit. Talking to these guys would be like talking to the cows. They wouldn't understand a thing he said.

The next few days were dedicated to getting the right clothes and adjusting to military life. Their sergeant, Curillo, was bilingual, and seemed determined to make life as miserable as possible. Chap scrubbed toilets and pained for home. Surprisingly, neither the scrubbing nor paining killed him. Over the next four weeks, he actually excelled.

The pre-dawn hours weren't hard. Chap had been getting up at 4:00 a.m. most of his life. The other guys were from Puerto Rico and the big city, and most found the early hours brutal. Some were friendly, but the majority seemed to resent Chap's ability to speak English.

On the rifle range, Chap didn't see targets, but groundhog noses at three hundred and thirty yards. He loved the M16. Weighing four pounds, fourteen ounces, it felt like it belonged in his arms. He took care of it as if the survival of mankind depended on how he treated his weapon.

But there was more to being a soldier than mastering the M16; there was an Apache officer named Asotto to contend with.

Asotto taught them weapons and hand-to-hand combat. The Apache's skill was fascinating, but Chap tried to stay out of his way.

One day during training, Asotto yelled at Chap and said, "Boy, you think you're tough?"

Chap looked behind him, but no one was there. Asotto addressed him.

"Yeah, boy, you. The blonde-haired pussy. Come here, boy."

With the hated blond-haired pussy name stinging his pride, Chap went forward, angry enough to overcome his dread of the officer and fight if he had to.

Asotto held the bayonet from his M16. "You want me, want to kill me? I'm gonna let you kill me, tough boy." He slapped Stone, sissy-like across the face.

The second slap bent Chap's head back and would leave a print.

Asotto walked a circle around Chap, taunting. "Try to kill me, tough man. Come on, pussy-boy."

Over the last weeks, Chap had been at bayonet practice for hours, and loved sinking it into the target. He could take this Indian.

All he had to do was lunge and Asotto would be dead.

"C'mon, sissy. C'mon, you big pussy. You think you're bad. Farmboy. You think you're bad. Farmboy."

Asotto slapped Chap again, and spit on him.

Chap lunged for the heart with his bayonet, just like they'd taught him to, just like he'd practiced a thousand times.

As his arm reached full extension, something smacked Chap just below the mouth. His teeth came through his lower lip. Asotto's arm closed around his neck, and the big blade pressed against Chap's throat.

"Farmboy," Asotto whispered, his breath steaming Chap's inner ear, "never get so angry your target can kill you."

The blade nicked Chap's throat with a sting. A warm trickle of blood crawled down his neck.

Asotto threw Chap down. He hit the ground hard and dabbed at the blood, stared at his fingers in disbelief.

"You've just watched a Perry Right," Asotto addressed the rest of the troops.

Chap put both hands on the ground. So it wasn't personal, he was just the monkey picked to prove a point. He was grateful to be able to take a deep breath. The terrible anger lessened, and he felt like a fool. He pushed the lip over his tooth and felt it break. The blood coming out of his mouth pissed him off again, but he didn't say a word. Sitting in the front row, a medic's bandage on his lip, Chap watched the Indian for the rest of the day.

Eight weeks later, Basic Training and Advanced Infantry Training concluded. Chap had maxed scores in his physical fitness test, maxed scores with the rifle, and mastered bayonet training.

His platoon had grown as a team. He'd been ready to hate the Puerto Ricans in his outfit, talking their crazy Spanish fast talk. Now they seemed like brothers.

The graduating recruits held a parade. The General congratulated them, told them they'd be receiving their orders that evening. Before long they'd make a journey and represent their fellow Americans in a proud and wonderful way.

Chap didn't really care. He didn't need the army to tell him to be proud of himself. Judging what he'd been through and how he'd come out, he was proud enough. And soon, he'd be traveling.

That evening, Chap kicked around with the other guys.

Sergeant Curillo called the entire platoon outside. "Soldiers, I hold in my hand your orders." Curillo put the men in quads and asked them to come to attention.

He called Chap Stone. After receiving his orders he fell back in line, while staring at the sheet of paper between his harden hands. "You are hereby ordered to report to Fort Lewis, Washington, for transportation to the Republic of Vietnam in the 25th Division, Infantry."

People died in Vietnam. They gave the weekly death count on the evening news, he thought.

Up front, Curillo grinned, obviously enjoying himself. "Gentlemen. If you do not agree with your orders at this time, there is an alternative. I want to introduce to you Sergeant Major Edwards."

Edwards walked forward. He had so much starch in his pants he didn't need bones in his legs. Chap could have tweezed a splinter in the mirrored shine of Edward's boots.

"At ease," Edwards barked. Edwards paced back and forth before talking and then took a spread-legged stance, his arms folded behind him. "If you think you're good enough, and you're ready for a challenge, and you don't want this bullshit Vietnam War, I have an option for you. Would you like to be one of the real few that have courage?"

Chap thought he'd already been made into the toughest soldier in the Army. What was this courage baloney?

"Would you like to become an infantry airborne?"

"Airborne?" Chap repeated. He weighed his options—airborne, Vietnam. Airborne. Vietnam. Airborne . . .

Edwards barked, "If you want to be considered, I repeat considered, for some of the finest organizations in the world, please fall out and go into the rec hall."

Chap looked down the line of men. No one moved. He stepped forward, squared his shoulders and headed for the hall.

Out of a company of ninety, only six guys waited for Edwards. Chap swallowed everything the sergeant had to say, then signed on the line. He'd saved his butt from Vietnam.

###

At 0400 hours the next morning, Chap and five more raw recruits were on a bus destined for Fort Benning, Georgia. Chap felt good about this ride. After sixteen weeks of training, infantry airborne would be a piece of cake.

At the fort, four drill sergeants met the bus. That was almost one sergeant per man. They each barked a litany of different orders—"Get down, get up, push up, sit up, jump, run."

"Push up, get down, sit up, get up, jump."

"Jump, run, get down, get up, jump."

"Run. Run. Run."

Puffing like a string of engines, Chap and the others were hustled to their barracks. The orders continued. "Shine those boots, stow that gear, make those beds."

"Man," Chap muttered, "I'm about to go nuts."

Nobody could make a decision before some new order was shouted in their faces.

The next morning, Chap fell into formation. He'd worked half the night just shining his boots. First thing the airborne sergeant did was welcome them to the new challenge.

"There're forty of you here today. By day's end, there will only be twenty. You who remain will know you are airborne material. Gentlemen, let's take a little run." The sergeant ran backward. Chap and the others fell in behind.

"Airborne . . . ranger . . . Vietnam . . . Charlie Cong . . . kill him now . . . kill him dead. Airborne . . . ranger . . . Vietnam . . . Charlie Cong . . . kill him now . . . kill him dead."

They'd started at six o'clock. When they passed the three-mile point, Chap's tired body let him know.

But the drill sergeant was barking orders, barking cadence, always running backward. "Airborne . . . ranger . . . Vietnam . . . Charlie

Cong . . . kill him now . . . kill him dead. Gonna take a little hike up a hill called Agony."

After ten miles, two had dropped out. Now the ground was rising, and Chap felt the pull in the front of his thighs, in his calves, a building pressure in his head, in his chest.

"Agony," was a five and a half mile grade. Chap's lungs burned as he sucked deep. "Airborne . . . ranger . . . Vietnam . . . " The incantation pulled each step from Chap's body, again, and again, and again.

###

Nine hours later, the running ended. Blisters burned the bottoms of Chap's feet. He felt dizzy, started to fall. Someone held him up, put a canteen to his lips. He drank it all and threw it back up. He drank again, only slower this time. When he looked around, eleven guys remained.

Three weeks later, training ended. The captain informed them it was time to learn what airborne really meant.

On the first day of jump, the C141 droned high. Chap made another check on his equipment. His hands felt for each item as he mentally listed—chute on his butt, emergency on his gut, M16 on his side, forty-two-pound pack on the back. "Why would I want to jump from a perfectly good airplane?"

The sergeant at the rear door called Chap's name. "Stand up, soldier. Stand tall." He was the same relentless sergeant that nearly ran

Chap to death. "What are you?" he barked.

"Airborne, Sir."

"Have you jumped?"

"No Sir."

"Will you jump?"

"Airborne, Sir."

"What's airborne, soldier?"

"Airborne . . . kill Charlie Cong . . . Vietnam."

"Airborne, jump!"

Without even thinking, Chap stepped into the clouds. Seven seconds later, he felt the static line pull as the chute opened.

He was finally free.

They took three more jumps that day. Three more times Chap soared, his feet pushing through the sky. Airborne infantry training was completed. Chap had earned his wings.

They had another parade the following day. Again, the officers told them what great and wonderful persons they were, but Chap barely listened. The feeling of completion melted all the way to his soul. If what he'd accomplished didn't make him a man, then he'd like to know what the heck would.

The following night, Sergeant Anderson told them to fall out. "Gentlemen, I have your new orders."

Each man was handed a slip of paper. "You are hereby ordered to report to Oakland, California, to the AP station there, for transportation to Ninetieth Replacement Center, Long Ben, Vietnam."

Chap packed his bag that night, thinking of all the things he'd learned. In the latrine, he gripped the cold polished end of the metal sink. He didn't know the guy in the mirror. Hard muscles covered the bones of his face. No roundness, no softness . . . no ponytail.

Over and over in his head ran the chant, the litany, his creed courtesy of the U.S. Army, "Vietnam . . . kill Charlie Cong . . . Vietnam."

It was January 1969, and there were no more options. This time Chap could go home for thirty days, and wait to see what he was really made of.

###

The bus pulled next to a bleak spot along the road. Holding his bag in front of him, Chap made his way to the front. In spite of the fourteen-hour ride, he still looked sharp in army dress greens with new PFC rockers on his shoulders.

The doors sighed as they opened. He stepped onto the road, waited for the quiet, and the smell of Neosho countryside.

He wanted to see Mom. The duffel bag rode his shoulder, and he jogged toward the house. Then he ran.

The December air made his nose and cheeks tingle. His breath steamed white before his mouth, but Chap didn't break cadence. He could see the smoke from their woodstove curling dark gray against a white sky. The black and white cows in the back pasture huddled in groups waiting to be milked. The homeplace wasn't much more than a tarpaper shack, but it looked good to him.

Chap reached the front porch, vaulted the stairs and flung open the green paint-chipped door.

Mom stood there waiting just inside the door. Chap took a wide step, ready to fold her in a hug, but she gripped his forearms, held him away, and looked him over, from close-cropped hair to the spit shine on his shoes.

Grinning, Chap stood for inspection.

"What have they done to my boy?"

He grinned. "Don't be looking at me like that, Mom. They made me a man, is all."

Slowly, she put her arms around his neck. "A man," She said in fun, though her smile was slow and sad.

Chap felt her spirit wrap around him, her warmth. The certainty of her love slid beneath his dress greens and he felt a lurch of emotion.

Mom pulled away first. "Best close that door, Chap. We don't want to waste any heat." She dug in an apron pocket for a pink tissue, turned away wiping her eyes and nose. "I've made some coffee, Chap. Come to the table so we can catch up."

It was warm in her kitchen. Chap took in every inch of the place, from the African violets growing in tin cans on the sill over the sink, to the old Coldspot refrigerator wearing a chocolate layer cake for a hat.

The linoleum was worn away in front of the sink and the stove. Avocado green Melmac dishes were stacked neatly inside the white metal cabinet Dad had ordered from Sears last Christmas. Mom liked red-and-white-checked towels. She used one now to lift the lid on a big pot. He smelled her spaghetti sauce.

This was the way he'd pictured her these months. He yanked out one of the yellow chrome chairs. How many times he'd run silver tape over the most recent splits in their vinyl upholstery. "You don't know how good it is to be here, Mom."

She brought two mismatched mugs of coffee to the table. One said, "Florida," from Aunt Betty's vacation. The other his dad had gotten free from the bank. "Are you home to stay, Son?"

Chap took a sip of the strong sugary coffee. "This is just leave time. They're shipping me away."

"Away? Well, where to?"

Chap didn't want to tell her yet, didn't want to bring the reality into this kitchen. He made small talk, and she told him some of the local news. Someone was pregnant. Someone got married. Someone passed on.

"Let's turn on the news for a minute."

Mom stared at Chap for long silent seconds. She nodded. "All right, Chap."

They carried their coffee to the living room. She switched on the small black-and-white TV set she was so proud of. Credits for *As the World Turns* rolled across the screen.

Shortly pictures of a wounded boy on a stretcher filled the small screen. GIs lifted him into a helicopter for transport to a MASH hospital.

Mom backed to her rocker, still holding her coffee. Chap sat on the couch, his cup within reach on the end-table, elbows on his knees.

Walter Cronkite gave the number of Americans killed in Vietnam that week, as five hundred forty-three.

She kept her attention on the tube. He didn't think she'd made the connection until he saw a tear roll down her cheek.

Chap went to her, knelt by the rocker, set her coffee on the table, and then took her hands. They felt slick, work-roughened. He pressed the loose, chapped skin on her knuckles. "It'll be okay, Mom. Nothing's going to happen to me."

He saw the trouble deep in her eyes, the eyes she'd told him would always be watching, wherever he went, whatever he did. "You're so young."

He laughed, not because he found her funny, but because he

hadn't expected her to say that. Didn't she see how grown he was now? "They don't want a bunch of old men over there, Mom."

Her chin trembled, and she shook her head, looked away, back to Cronkite. "What's so special about that place that we've gotta send our boys over there?"

He realized she'd asked herself this before, maybe since that first day when he hadn't come home.

"The army has taught me things you wouldn't believe. And you know I'm the best shot there ever was. I can handle myself. Everything will be fine."

Mom pulled her hands away, stood and crossed the room. But she didn't go in the kitchen. Before Chap could even get up from the floor, Mom went in her bedroom and softly shut the door.

### 

Chap had three weeks to spend with his family. When it was time to say goodbye, he shook Dad's hand. "Do what you gotta," Dad told him, not able to look him in the eye.

Mom hugged his neck. As always, Chap felt her spirit. She whispered, "Bring nothing home you wouldn't want to give to me, Chap." Her kiss punctuated her words.

Chap hoisted his duffel bag and started down the hill toward the spot where he'd catch the bus.

He wouldn't look back, could already see it—them standing

apart and alone, behind them the trees bare and harsh, the house chipped and sagging.

He let the rhythm of his footsteps start the chant. "I want to go to Vietnam. I just want to kill Charlie Cong. Your left, right, your left. Your left, right, your left. I want to go to Vietnam. I just want to kill Charlie Cong."

The bus was on time. Chap showed his ticket to the driver and took a seat near the aisle because he had no heart for the scenery. He was just another GI in a green uniform. Destination Ninety-third Replacement Station. Long Ben, Vietnam.

Across the aisle a little girl stared at him. Chap smiled. "You're a soldier," she told him.

"Yeah," he agreed. "I guess I am."

"You ever been in a war?"

Her mother told her to hush and leave the man alone.

Chap was glad he didn't have to answer.

# HILLSBORO, ILLINOIS, APRIL, 1968
# ROGER MURPHY
# CHAPTER 2

> "It's best to know who you are—but knowing who you aren't runs a close second."
>
> —Roger "Doc" Murphy

Roger Murphy walked to the mailbox, holding his breath. The stretched shadow of his five-foot-ten-inch frame shaded the metal box. He reached an oversized hand inside and grabbed the pile of letters.

Sorting through the stack, he mumbled aloud, "Mrs. James Murphy, Mrs. James Murphy, Mr. Murphy . . . Mr. Roger Murphy." There it was. Roger walked quickly in the house.

Looked like all his hard work—three years of straight A's, rising early to do a paper route, working construction on weekends with Dad—all his efforts were going to culminate in this letter from Penn State.

"Hey Mom!"

Mrs. Murphy came into the dining room from the kitchen.

"It's come, Mom. It's really here."

Roger passed his mother, and she followed him holding on to the silverware draining from the sink. He took a butter knife and made a careful surgeon's cut across the paper seam.

"Congratulations, you have been accepted on full scholarship as a pre-med student at the University of Penn State. Enclosed are documents you must complete to confirm your acceptance," he turned the volume up on the next word, "scholarship."
Roger looked up at the dropped ceiling he'd helped Dad install last winter. Wait till he went to school on Monday and told the hippies and jocks what he was going to do with his life.

Late Saturday afternoon, two friends from school, Dean and Dixon, came by the house. Dean started to complain about his Impala's lagging transmission, when Roger overwhelmed the conversation. "You guys aren't going to believe this. I got accepted in the pre-med program at Penn State."

They hooted and rapped Roger's back. He felt like he'd just made the saving touchdown at the homecoming game.

Dean said, "You know, Roger, we need to have a party. We gotta celebrate."

Dean and Dixon never asked Roger to party. Maybe they knew it wouldn't do them any good with the schedule Roger kept. More likely, Roger wasn't cool enough. He hadn't been since junior high, when he'd chose books and grades over sports and girls. Although the three had been friends since grammar school, Roger would have been history long ago if not for his well-lighted garage and a dad who allowed the boys to work on their cars, even use his tools if they were properly taken care of.

"We got to have us a party. You got accepted to Penn State, man, we gotta have us some F.U.N." Dixon bowed his back, stuck out his knees and pumped his arms and hips in sync.

"Yeah, we got to go to Belleville, to the Big Apple." Dean smacked Roger on the shoulder.

Roger laughed, chewed his bottom lip. "What's the Big Apple?"

Dean and Dixon fell against each other whooping and carrying on. Dean lowered his voice, "The Big Apple is a place where guys like us can get a drink. We can have us a good time, meet some chicks and have the best night of our lives."

Roger ran a hand over his square chin. He'd never done something like this before. School would be out in a couple of weeks. He wouldn't see Dean and Dixon for a long, long time. "Okay, man. What do I need to do?"

Dean patted the air, "Don't worry about nothin'. Just be ready at eight, and we'll pick you up. Be ready to have a good time."

###

At eight, Dean's horn blasted over the sound of his transmission from in front of the house.

Roger told his mom goodbye. Dad was in his recliner, reading the Hillsboro paper. "Son?"

"Yes, Sir?"

"You sure you want to do this?"

"We're just going out to have a good time."

"If you ever get in trouble with the law, don't ask me to get you out."

Roger expelled a long breath. "I've never been in trouble in my life. This is the first time these guys have asked me to go along. What's wrong with one night of fun?"

"You just remember what I said." Roger's dad flipped the paper in front of his face. Discussion over.

Dean's red and white '63 winged Chevy Impala sat in front of the house like a supersonic jet ready for takeoff. Roger climbed in the backseat. Any damper Roger's dad had put on his mood was quickly dispelled by the wild enthusiasm of Dixon and Dean. It was like nothing bothered these two, so why should he be any different?

Five miles down the interstate; Roger heard the pop of a can opener. Dixon lifted a foaming gold and white can of Falstaff over the front seat.

"Oh, no thanks," Roger mumbled.

"Go on. One lousy beer's not gonna hurt nothin'."

Roger took the lukewarm beer. He tasted a sip, and resisted a shiver. What did people see in this stuff? Tasted like sour dishwater to him. But it did make him feel kind of good to hold it, to raise it to his lips the way his friends did.

Tooling down Interstate 55 headed toward Belleville, Roger drained his first beer. And his second. They took Exit 21, hit a couple of side streets, and reached the Big Apple.

Teenagers filled the front parking lot. "We're gonna help you out, tonight," Dean said, clapping Roger on the back as they walked quickly to the front door.

Such camaraderie felt great. As they approached the entrance, Dean passed Roger someone else's driver's license. "Belongs to my girl's brother," Dean said out of the side of his mouth.

Roger quickly read the card. He buckled his knees and stooped his shoulders hoping to pass for five-foot-six.

The guy doing the carding waved them in with barely a glance. At the bar, Dean tipped the bartender three dollars. "My friend here needs something good. He's never been drunk before."

"Before now," Roger added. He was feeling good enough to jump on the bar and dance.

"Rootbeer Snapps," Dean announced, clinking his glass against Roger's.

"Not bad," Roger approved.

Another Falstaff followed. Another Snapps. Then Roger lost

count.

The night was a haze of drinking, pushing through the melee in the john, asking the best-looking girls in the place to dance and then asking the worst-looking dogs. Before long, someone thought to check the clock and realized it was after two. They knew they'd better head home.

Dean swore he was able to drive. Roger fell into the backseat and didn't move. It seemed like everything was gut-pumping funny. They could even laugh at nothing. Someone would start, and the other two joined in.

When Roger closed his eyes, he felt like he was on a giant turntable, going faster and faster. He pulled himself upright, tried to read the highway signs that whizzed past. "I gotta pee," Dixon slurred. "Stop the damn car. I gotta pee."

Abruptly, Dean pulled to the side of the interstate, jerking them forward, then back.

Dixon fumbled with the door handle and stumbled out. Dean shoved the Impala in park and got out too. Both boys staggered to a nearby light pole and started to go.
Watching them made Roger think it wasn't such a bad idea. He moved out of the car, and his head started to throb. He got as far as the pole, had his pecker in his hand, when someone tapped his back.

A state patrolman stood behind Roger. Dean and Dixon

convulsed with laughter. Roger was so shocked, he started to pee, wetting the patrolman's pant leg and shoes.

"Stop it, you dumb son of a bitch," the patrolman yelled, digging at his belt for the long black stick.

Dean and Dixon collapsed with laughter, but Roger watched the black stick, coming at him, sticking it in his face while the cop screamed, and screamed . . .

Then everything went black.

###

No one laughed on the way to the precinct, or in the cell at the station.

Roger didn't know what he'd done until Dean and Dixon told him about pissing on the patrolman's leg. He fingered the tender knob on his head from the billy club as a guard approached the cell.

"C'mon, kid, it's time to make your phone call." He unlocked the door, hoisted Roger to his feet, and dragged him out. Mixed emotions boiled inside Roger on the way to the phone. He'd never dreaded a confrontation more than the one ahead with his father, yet he knew Dad was the only one who could rescue him.

The receiver was sticky, and weighed five hundred pounds. He held it against his ear and, with the dread of the damned, dialed his home number.

One ring. Two. His father's sleepy, alarmed voice answered.

"Hello Dad, I . . ."

"Roger?"

"Dad, I'm in trouble. I'm at the county jail. It was all a mistake . . . can . . . can you come and get me?"

Roger closed his eyes tight, stealing himself for the bitter disappointment in his father's voice. He didn't realize the phone was dead until the dial tone hummed.

Slowly, he replaced the receiver. "He hung up," he told the officer, not able to look him in the eye.

"C'mon kid."

Head pounding, Roger kept pace with the officer as he led him back to the cage.

###

At nine-thirty the next morning, Roger heard the keys jingling, announcing the approach of the guard. "Got a court appearance, kid. Gotta see the judge."

Roger swallowed against a sore throat. Dean and Dixon had left with their fathers hours ago. Only he remained to face an uncertain fate, and he was mad.

"What for?" he asked himself.

The guard twisted the keys in the lock, jerked the door wide. "You're charged with a felony—disturbin' the peace, assault on a public officer."

"Assault?"

"You pissed on an officer's leg."

"That's not assault. I didn't hit him."

The cop gripped Roger's arm and led him from the cell. "It's still a felony, kid."

Roger tried to ignore the hoots from the other prisoners. "God, I'm in hell."

The bailiff led him nearer the courtroom. Resolute pain beat against the top of his head. He'd vomited on his shirt and in his hair, and the inside of his mouth felt like the scum side of a bucket. He'd peed and defecated in his pants, without memory of doing either one.

They waited in the back of the courtroom. When Roger's name was called, he shuffled forward like a homeless bum.

The judge was a little man, with a mop of iron gray hair, and eyes like probes of light, made for looking into people's souls . . . and condemning them.

Roger smelled himself, standing before the elevated desk. He felt like a heathen at the second coming. The tempo in his head drummed with such insistence, he feared passing out.

The bailiff whispered, "Don't laugh now, kid. You got the hangin' judge."

The judge banged the gavel and the bailiff read the charges. "Public drunkenness and assault." The way the judge scowled, it might as well have been "rape and murder."

"Did you assault someone, young man?"

The bailiff handed Roger's paperwork to the judge. "Says right here the charge is assault."

Roger squeezed his buttocks lest he would crap his pants with full knowledge.

The judge read the charges for himself and then expelled a sigh of disgust. "What are our young people coming to? Teens assaulting my police officers? I can't have that. How do you plead?"

He could fall on his knees and sob like a penitent baby—with a soiled diaper.

The judge grew impatient. "Are you guilty or not?"

"I don't know. I mean . . . I didn't do anything."

The judge repeated his request for a plea. He stacked his old wrinkled lips in a straight line waiting for an answer. Ten seconds passed, twenty. Roger tried to fumble an explanation, but nothing sounded worthy of mercy. He almost felt relieved when the judge smacked his gavel on a hard little circle of wood.

"You can either plead guilty now, and I may give you some leniency, or you can get a lawyer and come back. But in the meantime, I'm going to keep you locked in my jail for at least the next year."

To spend a year in jail meant he couldn't graduate. No graduation meant no scholarship to Penn State.

He tried to think, ran a shaky hand over his brow, and smelled the dried puke on his shirt. A guilty plea carried a possibility of leniency. Of course, he had to take it. "Well, young man? What's it going to be?"

Roger took a deep breath. "Judge, I'm sorry I did that to the officer. I didn't mean to, but I'm guilty."

The judge wheeled his chair back from his desk. Ten heartbeats passed. Twenty. "Maybe I've misjudged you just a hair," the old coot finally spoke. "Maybe you are regretful for your unlawful actions." Twenty-five heartbeats. Thirty. "I'll give you a choice of six months in jail and a felony record, or following the bailiff down the hall and enlisting in the United States Army."

Hope shot through Roger's lips in a rush of breath. He was going to medical school. It didn't equate with jail, with felony or with the Army? Roger swallowed hard, and tears distorted his vision. He had to think, think of a way out, but this old jerk wasn't going to give him one.

Anger overrode the headache and the smells, and the shame. Roger kept his eyes on the gavel. Damn his father. This was all his fault. Five heartbeats. Ten.

Through his teeth, he surrendered, "I'll take the Army."

The gavel cracked. "Case closed, strike it from the record."

The overweight bailiff grabbed Roger's arm and led him from

the room. "You know, you made a good decision, kid." The guy was popping stale Wrigley's gum. Roger wanted to punch him in his fat face.

The recruiter sat behind a table at the end of the hall. Some other kid was bent over, signing his life away.

The bailiff told the recruiter about Roger's case, his decision to join the Army—chew, chew, pop, pop.

The recruiter slouched in his chair and sucked his strong white teeth. "Tell you what, my man, I'm feelin' good today. Give you a choice. You can go in the infantry, artillery, do mortars, or be a combat engineer." He spread his arms wide. "What would you like your Army to be for you?"

"You know, Sir . . ."

"I work for a living, mister. I'm a sergeant."

"Sergeant then, I've been accepted to Penn State as a medical student."

The sergeant rubbed a finger against his bottom lip. " "How about if we take some battery tests, hot shot, see where you score the highest?"

"When, Sir?"

The sergeant straightened, reached for the briefcase sitting next to his chair, and sat it on the desk. "How about right now?" He clicked open the brass locks.

For two hours, Roger pushed through his headache and filled out the test. When time was up, the sergeant put the test in a stylus and punched through the correct scores. After a few minutes of examining the results he said, "You're right. You wouldn't be bad in medicine. Ever thought about being a medic? It's kind of like an understudy for a doctor."

It didn't matter now. He signed the paperwork. The sergeant said he'd get Roger a bus ticket to Fort Leonard Wood, Missouri, that very morning. "Why don't you take a shower, Doc, and the Army will take care of you."

True to his word, in less than an hour, the sergeant had a bus ticket and was sending Roger to basic training.

In twenty-four hours he'd gone from the happiest day of his life to the twilight zone. From immense hope to resignation. From feeling the pride in his mother's eyes to the sorrow in his dad's heart.

He wasn't even allowed to go home and get a bag.

### 

A few hours later, Roger arrived at Fort Leonard Wood, Missouri. A numbness spread to his limbs, making him feel disconnected, like he only watching what was happening now. A hand grabbed him by the collar of his shirt, another gripped the back of his belt. He was propelled to the front of the bus and tossed out the door.

For a good ten feet, he fought to stay upright. In the end, he landed hard on an elbow and knee.

Above him stood a black "Mr. Clean" in Army greens, an officer of the United States Army, crowned by a halo from the sun. "Boy, when I say get your ass off the bus, I mean it."

Suddenly, the numbness was gone. Roger Murphy reentered his life.

###

Only one thing lacked when Roger completed his training sixteen weeks later—heart. He did well at rifle, drill and bayonet, but his heart wasn't in any of it.

At the close of the graduation ceremony, they started to read orders. The word "Vietnam" was in the air—a word as joyless as cancer.

Roger's name was called and he went forward. Quickly, he glanced at the bold black print. Fort Sam Houston Medic's School, eight weeks training.

Many were signing on for additional infantry school, some for engineer's training, and others were headed for Vietnam. But Roger had the promise of eight big weeks of medical training. It looked weak in light of the full medical scholarship that had slipped through his fingers, but at least he'd be staying on American soil.

### 

Arriving at Fort Sam Houston, Texas, Roger located the induction center for the medic's school. The training the recruiting sergeant promised turned out to be nothing more than bandaging limbs and giving shots to dummies.

But the last two weeks, well, it turned serious. Roger's class was taken to the hospital to see firsthand the wounds of guys shipped home from Vietnam. As the nurse walked them down the hall, Roger looked through the squares of glass in the dormitory doors. Rows of bandaged, wounded GIs filled the beds.

The first ward they visited was for amputees. Soon as the nurse opened the door, deep-throated moans, high-pitched wails, and screams burst into the hall.

He smelled raw flesh beneath the antiseptic odors, and thought of Fulson's meat locker back home. Afraid he'd lose it, he struggled to look professional, like it didn't bother him to be amongst such suffering, like he saw it all the time.

The patient in the first bed had lost his arms and legs. Bandaged stubs poked from his shoulders, and hips. As the nurse explained how the medic in the field had acted to save this man's life, Roger met the soldier's dead-eyed gaze. In that look they shared a secret—the medic hadn't done squat. This guy died back in Vietnam.

Roger looked away first, embarrassed and sorry. He followed the group to the next bed, where the nurse flipped back the covers, just over a half a man. This guy had also lost a limb. His leg had been torn from its socket, ripping away half of the young hero's backside, and most shocking of all, his pecker.

The patient stared into space, too wounded to care that a bunch of bandage slappers and iodine painters gawked at what was left of his body.

Roger steadied himself against the iron footboard. The boy had red hair, like his sister Becky. And the same liberal sprinkling of freckles, and crooked front teeth. He didn't look old enough to vote. What kind of plans had he made for himself before this happened, what kind of dreams?

The nurse said, "The best thing we can offer these boys is our ability to get them to a surgeon as quickly as possible, usually within twenty minutes of being hit. Your job is to get the bleeding stopped, pack a bandage, and disinfect."

They couldn't help a guy like this. If it was Roger lying there half blown away, he'd rather be dead.

### 

By late December the long silver bus rumbled to a stop before the hardware store on the Hillsboro square. A lone figure got off, wearing the Army's dress greens and dragging a duffel bag.

Holly wreaths decorated light poles. Santa and his reindeer rode a wire stretched across the Main Street intersection, and Bing Crosby dreamed of a white Christmas from the courthouse's PA system.

Roger's mom didn't know he was coming, and neither did Dad. The Army gave the customary leave before they shipped him out.

During his training, Mom wrote several letters, telling him how upset Dad was over what had happened in court. She asked her son to please forgive his father's stubbornness.

Roger hoisted the bag to his shoulder and headed down the hill toward home. He hadn't gone a full block when a black pickup pulled to the curb.

"Hey Roger, is that you, man? Hop on in here, and I'll give you a ride."

Earl was a country boy, liked to run his dogs and drink a lot of beer. Roger threw his bag in the back of the truck before climbing into the dented pickup.

"You look good, in that uniform," Earl said. "How long you home for?"

"A few weeks."

"Headed home now?"

"Yeah. Just got in."

"I seen you get off the bus. Couldn't believe my eyes. Whole school knew they'd busted your ass and you joined the Army, but no one could believe it."

"Sometimes I can't believe it either, Earl."

Hillsboro looked the same, a blend of historic old houses and low-roofed, rectangular ranch homes. But its very sameness solidified how far removed Roger felt from the kid he'd been the night he'd left.

"What you been up to, Earl?"

"Just groovin'."

"Are you working?"

"Got laid off at the mine. Somethin' will come open in a few weeks. Least that's what they say at the Union hall."

Earl sounded so . . . free, like he owned himself, his future, Roger thought.

They pulled in front of the Murphy house. Christmas lights twinkled from the tree in the living room. Roger grabbed his bag from the bed and shook Earl's hand through the window.

"Think they'll ship you over to that Vietnam?" Earl asked.

"Looks that way." It sounded worse here, with the air of home around him, he realized.

"Kill one of them Commies for me."

Roger smiled. There was no way to answer that.

He pinged his finger against the mailbox and felt his heart wrench, had a flash of himself finding the letter from Penn State. But it didn't matter now. Roger couldn't afford to let it matter. He had three short weeks at home, and nothing could spoil it.

Mrs. Murphy was only four-foot-three. Folks wondered how such a small woman had such a big son. But what she lacked in stature she made up for in warmth.

He figured she'd seen him pull up. Nothing much got by her. She came running down the short sidewalk with her arms opened wide. Roger swung her around, and they both cried. He'd never had to comfort her before, but he did now. "It's okay, Mom. It's okay."

Dinner was like a birthday party. Mom served Roger's favorite fried chicken, mashed potatoes and gravy, and biscuits. Becky sat across from him, flashing her braces, smiling shyly like she didn't know him in dress greens with his hair short.

"I could fix you up with Regina Patton. She just loves a man in a uniform," Becky stuck her cupped hands way out in front of her chest and rolled her eyes, giggling.

He threw a biscuit at her. "I don't need any little kid's help getting a girl."

She laughed again. To Roger it was one of the happiest sounds. It was like old times.

Dad got home from work, and took his place at the head of the table. "Well," he nodded at Roger. "Looks like you're a soldier now."

Until this moment, Roger hadn't known if he'd fulfilled his mother's request and forgiven. He was raised to know his father was a man of his word. But he hadn't been eager to see him and hadn't been able to picture himself shaking Dad's hand.

"It's been a long time," Dad said, stretching his arm across the table, squeezing Roger's knuckles in a solid handshake.

Roger had risen to a half-stand to reciprocate. When they left off shaking, Roger felt awkward as he lowered to his chair. He didn't know what to say.

Dad suggested they pray. Roger didn't bow his head. He watched the others, as they were so eager to do as they were told to bow their heads, to open themselves.
He loved them, even his dad.

"Oh Lord, we come to you as one. May our lives be entwined with love. May we learn through one another's sorrows. May we hug each other's joy. May we entreat our children with gladness, and be forgiven where we fall short. Thank you for bringing back our son. Thank you Almighty Father." Roger stared at his plate in silence. If the old man broke down crying, he didn't know what he would do.

Finally, Dad said a strangled, "Amen." The family grabbed bowls and set to passing Dad the food. No one spoke for nearly a minute.

"I guess you're pretty proud of yourself in that uniform," Mom said. Becky laughed, and they grabbed at the empty comment like a life preserver.

Three weeks later they sat together watching the New Year's Day football game when the newsbreak came on talking about the Vietnam War. The last week of 1968, five hundred forty-seven American men had died.

With that report, all the fun in the room left.

### ###

Roger's last four days home passed quickly. His mother tried to make everything special, cooking his favorite foods, catering to him like an honored guest. Dad reminisced about his days in World War II, and his outfit, "Hell on Wheels." Roger knew Dad was proud, as proud as if his eldest son had graduated Penn State.

But he felt anxious to go, restless for what came next. They drove him to the bus stop. He would later catch a flight in St. Louis to Oakland, California.

It was a chilly winter morning. Roger kissed his mother. Dad shook his hand in a hard grasp, then pulled him close and whacked Roger's back so hard he coughed. Becky left tears on the side of his neck.

Behind Roger's smile, he wondered if he'd ever see them again.

When he reached St. Louis's Lambert airport, he located the ticket counter for the military. The woman behind the desk took his orders and those of the GI standing next to him. Roger eyed the guy's airborne wings and saw the stranger eye his medical corps badge.

"Where you heading?" Airborne asked.

"Ninetieth," Roger answered.

"Me too." He stuck out his hand, a paw as big as Roger's. "What're you called?"

"Roger Murphy."

The fella had a hundred-watt smile and a grip like Samson's.

"Folks call me Chap."

# VIETNAM, JANUARY 1969
# CHAP STONE
# CHAPTER 3

"Survival is a matter of being the best, numero uno—second place is reserved for the dead."

—Sergeant Hood, 1st of the 17th, Wolfhounds

The airplane droned on through most of the night. When they reached Oakland, California, nearly everyone wore a uniform, making Chap and Roger a part of something big and exciting.

They were directed to one of seven buses, each of which carried over seventy young men. After a short ride to the AP station, Chap and Roger joined the long line waiting to be processed. In turn, they were given bed linens and told to lie down. "The plane should leave tomorrow, so you need to sit tight, soldiers."

Carrying his gear, Chap followed the crowd to the converted airplane hangar, courtesy of World War II, that served as quarters.

He suddenly saw himself the way the little girl on the bus had seen him. The word "soldier" sank into his soul as though he'd been christened. Soldier. It wasn't a who, *the who* of himself was still Chap Stone, his mother's son, hunter, strong hands, hard worker. But *the what* overshadowed all that. He was a soldier, property of the United

States Army. He didn't belong to his mother, to himself, or to God, but to a giant green-colored fighting machine.

Did he have what it took to be the real thing—a real soldier? That was the big question.

Inside, it looked like a thousand people sleeping in each bay, with only two sinks and one stool to share. Good thing an army of portable johns stood outside the hangar.

Chap dumped his gear and made his bed. The atmosphere rivaled the Neosho library for quietness and sobriety. Quiet like that could get to a guy. He wanted to rest, but didn't want too much time to think. Roger had brought cards along, and they played several hands of poker to keep busy.

When sleep finally came, it was cut short by a messenger rudely calling their names. "Grab your bags and head out for the bus. Get ready for your turn in the barrel."

"The barrel" was an old-looking silver craft with no identifying marks. Rows of triple seats were on the right, doubles on the left.

Roger and Chap found two seats together. They looked forward to one another's company on the twenty-hour flight.

"I thought stewardesses were supposed to be good lookin'," Chap muttered to Roger as they stowed their gear.

"These two gotta be older than my mother."

"My mother's better looking," Roger agreed as they fell into their seats. "Guess I can scrap that idea about makin' it with one of them in the john," he smiled.

They were given last-minute instructions by the women. One of them assisted Roger in buckling his seatbelt. Chap shook with laughter.

"You got yours done right?" the attendant snapped at Chap.

"Yes ma'am," he was quick to answer. When she moved on, Chap elbowed Roger in the ribs. "Should've grabbed her while you had the chance."

As the plane taxied down the runway, Chap and Roger laughed away all the tension from the layover. They were finally on their way.

Next stop—Hawaii.

### 

Chap was too tired to care about the in-flight movie. He tried to settle down and sleep like Roger, but again the tension was building. If he had to go to this godforsaken country, he'd just as soon get there and do the job.

Eight cramped hours later, they arrived in Hawaii. Chap disembarked in the rain. He breathed the humid Hawaiian air and followed the others into chow. The USO provided sandwiches. Chap downed two before a voice crackled from an overhead speaker. They needed to board their flight.

A new set of disappointing flight attendants replaced the last.

As the plane rumbled for takeoff, the stewardess went over the check list.

"Where do we stop next?" Chap asked.

He watched the stewardess's lips form the words beneath her faint brown mustache. "We'll stop at Midway."

"How long is that?"

"About seven hours."

Chap sank in his seat, shot a look of disgust Roger's way. "Seven more hours in this tin can."

As they crossed the ocean, Roger and Chap swapped stories. Chap related how he'd gone to Kansas City for a physical, and didn't make it home until Christmas. Roger shared how he'd gone out one night to celebrate a full medical scholarship and ended up with eight weeks of first aid training and a ticket to Vietnam.

"You know, this is the first time I've been able to laugh at the whole thing," Chap said, shifting around on the seat, trying to get comfortable.

"I'm going to be a doctor someday, I've promised myself that. Vietnam is a temporary setback."

Chap studied Roger for a moment. He was a quiet guy, but underneath there was something to him, something strong.

###

At Midway, the GIs unloaded and the plane refueled. The layover lasted two hours. Once they reboarded and were in the air, the stewardess informed them it was six and a half hours to Okinawa. Okinawa was the last stop before Vietnam. After going through the same routine, they headed for Bien Hoa.

Other planes could be seen gliding in as Chap's flight approached the base. They circled and circled, waiting for their turn to land. Inside the plane, no one spoke until at last they were going down.

Chap strained toward the window to watch their approach. Suddenly, on the left, an explosion of gray smoke erupted from a building. Their plane veered sharply away from the airstrip, abandoning its landing. Gear from the cargo bins fell on top of their heads.

Roger gripped Chap's arm, trying to share the view. "What are we in for now?" he asked low.

"Damn if I know," Chap answered with his guts in a knot. Silently, he prayed to set his feet on solid ground, even if it was Vietnam.

"We have to make another pass," the pilot spoke loudly over the intercom. "Don't worry. This is just somebody's welcome wagon. They usually make a little noise, then bundle up and leave."

Chap eased his shoulders against the seat. "I wasn't worried, were you?"

He and Roger expended their pent-up nerves in stilted laughter.

The pilot made the final pass, and this time, nothing happened. The plane landed smoothly and without incident. "Welcome to Vietnam," the stewardess spoke over the intercom. "Please walk down the stairs carefully. We'd like to see you on the return flight home next year. Good luck, gentlemen."

Chap followed Roger down the aisle. As soon as he stepped from the plane, a fierce smell assaulted his nose. "I'd say that's somewhere around a feed lot and a hog pen."

"With a little rotten cabbage tossed in," Roger agreed, looking over his shoulder.

With the smell came tropical heat-oven air with the dampness of a sauna added for spice. Following a private first class across the airstrip had rivulets of sweat crawling down Chap's back.

The terminal was in an abandoned building. The boys were quiet as they were processed. Roger followed Chap's lead to the old school bus they rode to the base. The heat moved from stifling to suffocating as Chap climbed into the bus. Mistakenly, he assumed the sight of closed, barred windows meant air conditioning.

"Hey, open the windows," someone yelled.

"Those windows are welded shut, boys. Can't take the chance on Charlie tossin' in a bomb and fryin' your little behinds." The driver seemed nonplussed over the heat, like he'd been a part of this scene many times before and even enjoyed it.

"My behind is fryin' anyway," Chap said to Roger.

"Man, mine too." Roger wiped his dripping face.

Ten smothering minutes later, they arrived at Ninety-third Replacement Station. The first sergeant they encountered was a woman. She looked at Chap's 201 file. "You'll do fine, soldier." She pointed him to the next line.

They were told to unload their bags. Half the stuff Chap brought from the states had to be mailed back home.

Each was issued clean clothes and canvas boots. Then there was another line, and another. Chap shifted his weight from leg to leg, trying to work out some of the kinks from the long flight. Sweat rolled into his eyes, down his back, while coloring his shirt, making it stick. He breathed like he'd run a mile, quick and shallow. He not only smelled the smells, he tasted them.

Finally, they handed Chap a bag. "You'll sleep here tonight, and they'll be along to pick you up."

"Who will?" he asked.

"Whoever gets through . . . 'Cruit."

Chap hadn't heard that handle before. It stung a little. He followed Roger to the bunks. They talked, played cards, tried to sleep, but the heat kept them awake. The smells burned their noses, made their eyes water, pulled the walls in close.

In the morning, the two hundred new arrivals from Chap's

plane were lined up, each by MOS, or job. Infantry was on the end, engineers next, truck drivers next, and so on to the last man. The men were a mixture of nearly everything the United States Armed Forces had to offer, but there weren't more than five or six of any one specialty.

"Hey, good luck, Chap." Roger needed to join the group of medics at the other end of the line.

Chap shook Roger's hand. "Hang in there, man. We'll run into each other again."

With the nervous anticipation of guys going on a first date, they waited for their rides. Finally, a five-quarter jeep with an M-60 in back pulled close to the building. Two guys jumped out. The white one, a sergeant, had a mad-dog look. A rough beard grew on his chin, and the neck of a whisky bottle poked from the top of his shirt pocket. The black man was a tall skinny kid about twenty or so with his pants rolled up to his thighs, and his boot laces pulled wide. Didn't look like any soldier Chap had seen before. "Chap Stone, front and center," the sergeant yelled. "Murphy, Doc, front and center. Ronald Wilkens, front and center."

"Welcome, newbies," the sergeant continued, the alcohol on his breath noticeable at three yards. "Welcome to the First of the Twenty-seventh. You are officially part of the Wolfhounds." The sergeant went inside the building, and the black kid leaned indifferently against the jeep.

Chap caught Roger's glance and gave him a smile. Whatever they were ahead for, Roger was part of it, too. What luck.

The other kid, Wilkens, looked about sixteen, too young to be a soldier. He had thick black hair and a baby face without a hope of a whisker.

Chap introduced himself, shaking Wilkens' hand. "Friends call me R.W.," the kid informed him. Said he trained in Fort Polk at South Fork.

"How'd you do?"

"Just made it," R.W. admitted.

Chap liked him for his honesty.

The sergeant returned. "Listen boys, want you to get in this truck. You watch, listen, and keep your mouths shut so I can get you there alive."

All three grabbed their bags, threw them in back, and prepared for what Chap felt would be the ride of their lives.

The first significant place they passed was the military post at Bien Hoa. The second was Long Ben, where they picked up boxes of C-rations.

"Where're we headin' to?" Chap asked a mile down the road from Long Ben.

Sergeant Hood slammed on the brakes and jumped out. He reached Chap double quick, blasting his alcohol breath in Chap's face. "I told you to shut your mouth if you want to live, you dumb mother!"

"Yes . . . ," Chap swallowed hard, nodded, ". . . Sir."

Chap didn't breathe until the sergeant was back behind the wheel. With a crunch, Hood shifted the gears, leaving tracks on the road as he peeled away.

Before Chap's heartbeat had slowed to normal, they came to a crossroads. The sign pointing left read, "Saigon, twelve miles." Right said, "To Hell."

Sergeant Hood squealed the tires as they made a sharp right turn.

### 

The road opened onto a smooth, modern four-lane. But the illusion of being stateside lasted only three miles. The road began to taper until the long limbs of the jungle pressed close, smacking their faces and arms as they sped past.

Hood drove thirty-five or forty, but it seemed like sixty. Macabee hollered, "Where you guys from?"

They guessed it was all right to answer. Each told him what state they hailed from. R.W. threw in a little more, told him his full name, how he'd been called after his daddy.

Macabee flicked a cigarette over the side. "Don't ever tell me more than I want to know. Gimme a handle, something short and sweet."

"R. W.'s what my friends call me."

Macabee nodded like he could live with that. "We're heading for a firebase called Black Horse."

An hour later, they approached an ancient bridge. A Vietnamese man rode a rickety bicycle close to the right side, causing Hood to slow the jeep.

The sergeant let the heel of his hand ride the horn. The old man peered over his shoulder, wobbling like a kid riding a bike for the first time.

"Dung lai!" he cried, a homemade cigarette hanging from his lips. "Dung lai!"

The old man's black silk pajamas caught the sun. His eyes looked worried beneath the brim of his cone-shaped hat. Age and disease had twisted the hand he waved at Hood.

Why harass an old guy like this? He'll be off the bridge soon enough, Chap thought.

Hood and Macabee put their heads together, conversing in low tones. After a few seconds, Macabee sat straight. "How long's it been since you killed a gook?" He spoke to Hood in a deep southern drawl.

The sergeant took his left hand off the steering wheel and counted out the number of days since his last kill. "Too long."

Hood shoved the five-quarter out of gear and jumped out of

the truck. He took the whisky bottle from his shirt pocket, unscrewed the top, and drank deep. He swallowed hard.

"Dung lai!" the papa-san called as Hood approached. The bike was still between his legs.

Hood waved his arms and yelled at the old man. Chap didn't know where such quick rage had come from.

"Kill the old bastard and be done with it," Macabee called, seeming tired of the whole thing.

Things slowed to a surreal pace. Hood slapped the holster at his side. His .45 caliber pistol flashed as he yanked it free. The sergeant turned once more to look at Macabee. Anger twisted his face. He turned back to the old man and placed the weapon squarely against his temple.

The papa trembled, hard enough to rattle the large baskets straddling the rear wheel. He screamed in Vietnamese and scrunched his neck into his shoulders. The .45 cracked and the old man's head lurched to the right. The cone hat flew from his head, and a trail of bright red bits sprayed into the dazzling sunlight.

His head rebounded toward Hood, flinging gore against the sergeant's face. Hood snorted like a bull, wiping frantically at his cheeks.

The body crumpled onto the bridge. Hood's boot slammed into the papa's limp body. He kicked the lifeless form again and again.

He snorted, kicked, and shouted profanity.

When he was tired of kicking, he walked in a circle, still angry, talking to himself now. And then he bent at the waist and rested his hands on his knees. The gun was still in his hand. He stayed this way, head hanging, breathing, for a long minute.

Finally, he straightened and holstered the weapon. Swiftly he bent and took hold of the dead man's arms. He dragged the body to the rail and hoisted it over the side. A quick splash followed.

Chap thought of his baptismal, being dunked in the pond by their pastor, coming up out of the water, his mom waiting on the bank with a towel, her face shining with love.

Hood pitched the bicycle over the railing, then kicked each of the old man's scant possessions into the river. He watched as they drifted to the water. Again he stayed bent, hands on his knees, panting. It seemed like the rage had stooped his spine, boiled it soft. Chap jumped when the sergeant lifted his head and screamed. It was a raw, primitive sound coming all the way from his belly like a warrior.

For a full minute, Hood stayed that way. When he straightened, he staggered. Then he sniffed and wiped his nose on his sleeve. Chap saw the dried flecks still on his face, and looked away, sickened.

"Better now, hero?" Macabee asked as Hood climbed behind the wheel.

"Don't mean nothin'. Gooks ain't human no how."

Macabee's laughter was high-pitched and wild. It rocked his body and he stamped both feet on the floorboards.

Chap pulled hard to fill his lungs. Macabee's laughter seemed as heinous as the murder. R. W.'s face was pale, beaded with sweat. Doc's lips trembled, like he had things to say but no words. In their eyes was mutual confirmation. That sign back at the crossroads didn't lie. They were in hell.

Hood squealed the tires past the warm, red scene of the murder. Chap whispered apologies to an old man's soul and to God. Macabee shoved an eight-track tape into his portable player. Rock and roll blasted from the speakers as the jeep roared toward the base.

### 

For two hours, they rode down the long dusty road in silence. Finally, around 1800 hours, the jeep reached a place that looked like a quarter mile of nothing wrapped in barbed wire.

Hood stopped at the gate. A guard approached, his uniform surpassing Macabee's for violations.

He sported a brief Ho Chi Minh mustache, and thin scraggly chin hairs. The Little Rascals would have envied his hat. Hippie beads swung from his neck. Even the Salvation Army would have rejected his raggedy clothing, and his boots hadn't had a drink of polish in about a year. Chap wondered what army this guy hailed from. Certainly not the same one he'd trained under.

The guard staggered to the jeep. "Is he sick, or wounded, or what?" he asked. Chap had never seen such a performance. The guy couldn't even speak clearly.

Hood exited the vehicle. He knocked the soldier on the ground and kicked his behind. "Damn you, Rabid. You're high as a jet."

In spite of the vicious kick, Rabid smiled and muttered agreement.

"Open the gate you miserable screw-up."

Rabid took his time getting on his feet. He stumbled to a level himself, and shoved it enough to motivate a block and tackle system. The razor wire gate lifted and the jeep shot forward.

"You boys gotta know now," Hood spoke loudly over the roar of the engine: "You're either a juicer or a head. If you're a head, keep away from me. If you're a juicer . . . we'll have a drink."

They were nearly unseated when the sergeant, obviously upset, slammed on the brakes and parked the five-quarter.

"We gotta go see the old man," Hood said.

"Who?" R.W. asked as they scrambled to get their gear.

"We gotta see the man in charge, you moron. The captain."

"What place is this?" Chap asked Hood.

"I told you, ass-brains, this is Black Horse. We should line you 'cruits up and shoot you the minute you step off the plane."

Chap stared at the back of Hood as he led them to the captain.

What an arrogant, murdering bastard, was all he could think of at this moment.

Hood took them down to a bunker marked CO. When they entered, all three lined before the captain, briskly clicked their heels, and saluted.

"Sergeant Stone reporting as ordered, Sir."

R.W. and Doc did the same.

How Chap wanted to tell the captain what Hood had done on the bridge. How he wanted to turn this bastard in and see him get hell.

"At ease, gentlemen," the captain said. "Rule number one. Outside of this bunker, you never, and I mean never, salute an officer. Do you understand me, Sergeant Stone?"

"Yes Sir. Why Sir?"

"Because I told you so, soldier."

"Sir, yes Sir."

Peripherally, Chap saw Hood on his left, hand covering his mouth, stifling laughter. It wouldn't be good to lose it in the first hour, but he didn't know how much more he could take.

"Hand me your orders, gentlemen." The balding captain, a short, compactly built man, looked at their orders. "You have been assigned to the First of the Twenty-seventh. Do you know what you're here for?"

R.W. said, "To follow orders, Sir."

"Where'd you come from, soldier?"

"Fort Polk, Louisianna, Norfork, Sir."

"How about you, Stone?"

"Fort Bragg, Sir."

"And you, Doc."

"Fort Sam Houston, Sir."

"Well, welcome to Hell, boys. You are in an infantry company. You are going to be assigned long-range missions. Now, I've got just one question, gentlemen. Do you want to go home alive?"

R.W. looked to Chap for help before responding, "Sir, yes Sir."

"Do you want to go home altogether, or do you want to go home in pieces, Sergeant Stone?"

"Altogether, Sir."

"Then you will do what Sergeant Hood tells you, when he tells you, and how he tells you. From this point on, he is the only way you are going to survive. Do you understand me?"

The vision of Hood, brutally and heartlessly shooting an old man on a bicycle blazed in Chap's mind. Now he was supposed to be his hero.

The captain looked at Stone as if divining his thoughts. "Soldier, Hood has been here four years. He eats, breathes, sleeps, hates gooks twenty-four hours a day. The only way you will go home in one piece and not in a body box is by listening to what he has to tell you. Do you understand?"

"Sir, yes Sir," Stone replied.

"Any further questions?"

None of the three responded. The captain turned to Hood. "Hood, take the doc to the medic's bunker and put the other two in your squad. How many you got?"

"I'm two short. Got nine, need eleven."

"Have to make do. Uncle Sam's not sending them over fast enough." Captain Collins got close to Hood's face. "Hood, don't kill them on the first night. Do you understand?"

Hood came to attention and saluted, "Yes, Sir."

The short hair on Chap's neck bristled when he heard the captain's words. *Kill them?*

They walked out of the bunker, into the last few minutes of twilight, and waited while Hood took Doc to the medic's hootch.

"What'd he mean about killin' us?" R.W.'s eyes were troubled.

"No telling with that maniac," Chap muttered, watching Hood's approach.

"This way," Hood motioned as he passed.

The sergeant led them to a bunker, a hole in the ground with sandbagged walls, hot as a pit for a pig roast. The latest tenant, a cat-sized rat, squeezed out through the corner.

"This is home for the next year, boys."

Chap was too mad to speak, too shocked, too unwilling to give Hood another reason to laugh.

"What do we sleep on?" R.W. asked.

"We'll get you some cots in a few minutes, man. Don't worry, this is the best place you could be. 'Fore you know it, this place will be heaven."

As promised, the cots arrived. Hood left Chap and R.W. to set up house. They put their cots together, then decided to cover them with their silk poncho liners. The silk didn't seem to cling to sweat-drenched skin.

From above, someone hollered, "Chow time." Other than Roger landing in the same outfit, this was the best news Chap had received since arriving in Vietnam.

They headed toward the mess tent, but something was missing. Chap breathed deep. "I don't smell anything."

"That's a pretty good observation, soldier."

Chap hadn't realized that Hood was walking behind, the same obnoxious smirk on his face.

"How can you have chow with no smell?" Chap asked, too hungry to put up with any more games.

They entered the tent. "You ain't opened up the can yet, son."

Hood clapped Stone hard on the shoulder and squeezed ahead.

Someone threw Chap an olive-colored can of C-rations. He grunted as it hit his chest. Bold black letters stamped on the lid read, "Scrambled eggs and ham."

R.W. had the same. So did Doc.

"Hey look at this, boys, turkey!" Hood called out. Another guy said, "Ham."

"You newbies better get the lead out of your butts if you're gonna get the good stuff." Hood stuck a thick chunk of white meat through the middle of his grin.

They opened the cans and Stone poked a spoon in the cold eggs. The smell reminded him of dogfood. Holding his breath, he took a bite. "God, that's awful," he told Doc and R.W. "Like eatin' a glob of cold shit."

Hood and the rest of the men snickered. R.W. tried to choke his down. His cheeks reddened like he'd been slapped and his eyes watered. Doc hadn't even opened his. He settled for a pack of crackers and peanut butter.

"Don't worry, Chap, we'll get it all figured out. Then it'll be our turn to laugh." Doc bit into a cracker, obviously savoring every crumb.

Motivated by fierce appetite, and wanting to deny Hood the pleasure of seeing him go hungry, Chap finished off the rations, and so did R.W.

Hood made a point of rubbing his satisfied stomach as he stood and rapped his knuckles on the table. "All right, you newbies, pay attention. These guys are your family for the rest of the time you'll be here. First up, this is Hatti."

Hatti's skin was a rich red-brown. Handsome and well built, he had the features and dark hair of an Indian. Chap stood. Whatever was coming, he preferred it on his feet.

"Where you from, boy?" Hatti sauntered close.

"Missouri."

"Farmboy?"

"That's right."

"So am I." Hatti stuck out his hand. "Glad to see you."

Chap was so relieved, he gave Hatti's arm a healthy pump.

Hood slapped the back of the guy who'd yelled, "Ham."

"This here son of a bitch is Sutherland."

Sutherland was tall, about 6′2″, a thin guy with fair coloring and eyes so wide they nearly reached his ears. Sutherland blew kisses at the newbies.

Chap lowered to his seat. It didn't pay to relax his guard for a second. Sutherland took the empty chair next to R.W. He grabbed R.W.'s thigh and squeezed. Hood and the rest of their new family roared.

R.W. was out of his chair like he'd been stung on the butt. "That ain't funny."

"Aw, come on back, newbie. We're lonely here," Sutherland whined.

"You ain't lonely for me."

Everyone laughed. Sutherland moved into R.W.'s chair, next to Chap. He put his hand on Chap's knee and slid it along his thigh. Chap leaned over and licked his ear.
Sutherland jumped away, "Hey man, what's wrong with you, sicko?"

Chap grinned. Now Hood and the others laughed and jeered at Sutherland. After eating slop for supper, Chap felt like he'd won something for a change.

Neil, a skinny blond-haired guy from Louisiana, was named Towhead. Hagland, the man who hated everyone, didn't get up to shake hands. He had an athlete's confidence and a grin that made Chap think he was up to something. Gonzales, nicknamed "Speedy," picked his teeth with a bayonet. His upper arms were the size of Chap's calves. He put forth an arrogance as inviting as a skunk's scent. When he caught Chap looking at him, he got on his feet. He looked anxious for trouble. "You lookin' at me, man? You want somethin' from me?"

"No, man. I was admiring your knife."

Before Chap had completed the word, "knife," Speedy threw the weapon. It stuck between Chap's open legs, three inches from his privates.

"They call me Speedy for a reason," Gonzales explained. "Understand, white boy?"

Chap understood. He understood these guys were a real bunch of nuts. He pulled Gonzales's knife free and handed it over. "Here you go, Speedy."

When Gonzales tried to stare him down, Chap didn't flinch, didn't look away. This made Gonzales smile.

French Fry looked about fourteen years old, and couldn't weigh more than a hundred thirty pounds soaking wet.

With most of the introductions over, Hood said, "Let's have us a goodwill drink. What you newbies want—beer?"

"Sure," R.W. said, "What you got?"

"Black Label or Falstaff."

"Oh, man," R.W. rubbed his hands against his knees, "Falstaff." Doc took the same.

Hatti came over to Stone. "Want a beer?"

Chap's stomach was unsettled from the traveling, the murder he'd witnessed, and the lousy food. The last thing he wanted was a hot beer. "I don't mess with kiddie shit. I only drink hard stuff."

"Like what?"

Chap tried to think of what his dad kept in the cabinet back home. "My daddy grew up drinking Old Granddad. That's all I ever drink, too. If you had some of that, I'd be glad to drink with you, but . . ." Chap shrugged.

Hatti straightened and looked over his shoulder at Hood. "What do you think, Hood? Is it worth it?"

"I don't see why not," Hood answered. "Go get First Sergeant Top. He's got the Old Granddad."

Chap rubbed a hand over his chest, trying to erase the dread. Who would've thought these guys had Old Granddad in the middle of the jungle?

In a few minutes, First Sergeant Top arrived with a bottle of Old Granddad and Southern Comfort.

"Which would you rather have, soldier?"

"Well, Sir, what would you recommend?" Chap asked.

"Say you've had Old Granddad before?"

"Yes Sir."

"Let's have some Southern Comfort and welcome you to the First of the Twenty-seventh in style."

They also offered the hard stuff to R.W. and Doc. Both boys held up their dark brown bottles of Falstaff. "We got beers already. We just can't mix it."

Top handed the bottle to Chap. "Take a drink, son."

Chap tilted the bottle to his lips and took a great, big, long, and he hoped manly, drink.

It tasted like cough syrup with a kick. It wasn't bad on the tongue, but it set his whole digestive system afire, igniting those C-rations to full boil. Chap coughed and sputtered. "G—God, this stuff is . . . good. *If I don't puke.*"

The rest of the group started laughing and joking and passed the bottle around having a good time. Stone took a drink every time the bottle came his way. It went from Falstaff to Black Label to Old Granddad for R.W. and Doc. Before they knew it, the newbies were so drunk they could hardly stand.

Stone fell hard against the ground. He knew R.W. was already sick and heaving. Doc hadn't moved in a while.

Nausea engulfed Chap; he prayed to die. He had no concept of his arms or legs, just his gut, and the deep clenching waves of sickness. He heard the laughing, every time he retched, but didn't care anymore. Nothing mattered but release from the misery.

Laughter exploded close to his ear. Vaguely, Chap was aware of being dragged to his cot. He opened his eyes enough to see Hatti dumping R.W. atop the poncho liner.

That was all Chap remembered, until the fire, the terrible fire that burned his pecker. Was it Gonzales's knife? Had it found its mark, sliced his privates to shreds?
Chap kicked and thrashed, staggered to his feet, but fell on his face when he tried to walk. His pants shackled his ankles, and he kicked

free, scrambling to his feet.

"My dick's on fire! My dick's on fire!" R.W. screamed as he ran up the stairs behind Chap.

Someone handed Chap a Coke. "Pour this on your pecker."

Chap went down on his knees. He then fell on his back, pouring and pouring the Coke between his legs, feeling the war between blisters and ice, seeing a bright flash, the second coming, or maybe a camera. He didn't care, only wanted relief.

R.W.'s screams grew distant. "He's headed for the shower," someone said. " Damn, he climbed on top of his makeshift bunk and fell in."

"That lineament won't come off unless he uses soap," someone said between choking laughter.

"Damn it, Hagland. That gook stuff'll eat through your hide if you're not careful. You must've poured the whole bottle on these boys," said Top.

Chap rolled on his side and lay in a fetal position. If he lived through this night, he'd pay these bastards back.

Hood's voice cut through Chap's thoughts. "Okay boys, towel 'em off, have the medics check 'em and put 'em to bed."

### 

The following morning, Stone awoke, pain tearing through his head if he dared to move. By degrees, he tried to sit up, but dry heaves knocked him flat. Everytime he raised his head, he threw up.

"God," Chap prayed, "if You'll let me get through this morning, I promise I won't do this to my body again."

He tried to stand up, but his legs felt boneless and heavy. The medic's hootch awaited, only one hundred yards away, cool and with aspirin. Might as well have been the other side of the world.

Chap inched his legs over the side of the cot. Slowly, the heaving subsided. Like a ninety-year-old man, he rose to his feet, and one small step at a time made his way toward the blistering patch of sunshine.

Hood and Macabee sat outside their bunker cleaning weapons. Another soldier, Sutherland, smoked a cigar. Gonzales sharpened his knife. Two mama-sans washed clothes in drums of water. Chap's knees buckled and he went down hard. Everyone laughed.

Doc appeared like a guardian angel and assisted Chap to the cool medic's hootch. Gently, he helped Chap lie down.

"Man, you're going to have to take care of yourself."

Chap looked at Doc with eyes of gratitude. "Thanks."

He slept the rest of the day in the hootch. Doc took care of him and brought him food. Chap thought to himself, "This is what Doc's meant to do." This is who he is and he knows it. He was grateful for Roger's quiet loyalty, his kindness that reaffirmed Chap's humanity.

By the time the duty roster came two days later, Chap had recovered from his initiation into the Wolfhounds. He and R.W. were taken to the supply area and issued their TA50—all the gear they needed for survival.

The following morning First Sergeant hollered, "Got patrol to go. Let's rock and roll. Get your ammo, two hundred rounds each. You're gonna be out for at least three days. Let's go."

Chap had never known the sudden onslaught of fear like he was learning here. Fear in the barrel when he'd seen the building blow. Fear in the jeep with Hood, fear when he'd heard the captain use the word "kill," and fear now with the thought of his first patrol.

They fixed their pistol belts and backpacks in silence.

"Three days," R.W. said, dark circles still under his eyes from their induction.

"Yeah, well, this is what we trained for, right, man?" Chap nudged R.W. like a big brother, feeling the stiff set in the younger man's shoulders.

They put their steel pots on, adjusted straps on their backpacks, walked outside in new fatigues, and stood in line.

Top spoke loudly, as if they were a company of one hundred, instead of nine. "Sergeant Hood has your orders. You'll relieve First Platoon in the Listening Post zone. Repeat, this is an LP zone. 'Listening Post,' for you dipstick newbies. Does not mean free kill. Does not mean shoot, does not mean holler, does not mean sleep. Does mean you listen and report back on the radio. That's it. Do you have that?"

*The Longest Monday*

Sergeant Hood turned to his men. His gaze went from Chap and R.W., over the other seven, then back to Chap and R.W.

"You pathetic ass-dumb 'cruits listen up. Stone, you have exactly two minutes to remove anything that rattles, clangs, beats, pings, taps, or makes any noise. Get it off your person. Do you understand?"

"Yes, Sir."

"That goes for you too, R.W. Go."

They ran back to the front of their bunker, threw off their steel pots, canteens, and everything else. They came back a second time.

"Newbies," Hood roared. "What are you going to drink?"

"You told us to get rid of anything that rattles or pings, Sergeant," R.W. reminded.

"Just the canteen container. You're gonna need some water out there, boy. Get rid of that steel pot," he knocked hard on R.W.'s helmet. "Put your soft cap on—the boonie hat, dumbshit."

R.W. and Chap ran back to their gear and made the adjustments before returning to the line.

Hood stepped close to R.W. and whispered, "If you want to come back alive, listen to me carefully. I'm your mother, I'm your father. Do what I tell you. Understand, boy?"

"Yes, sir."

Hood pulled a map from beneath his shirt and motioned for the men to gather around. "Look, all we're going to do is relieve First

Platoon. We're going to set up an LP. Stone, you'll carry the P25. R.W., you get to be the M60."

R.W. looked upset. "Why me?"

"You're the newbie, aren't you?"

The M60 was a machine gun that weighed about nine pounds. Every man knew it was a hog to carry. With the exception of Hood, everyone carried an M16. Hood preferred a shotgun, a model 97 Winchester with an extended tube and five rounds of ammo.

Chap begrudgingly admired the gun and Hood's pluck to think for himself. He well knew that Hood had a dangerous side, but going into the jungle with him in charge was more comforting than disquieting.

"Let's go, guys. Let's load 'em up. Let's go." Hood ran one last check. He pulled every tag, every bead, checking every detail on every man. The platoon left the safety of the compound and headed east.

###

In silence, they crossed a long clearing. Hood motioned for the men to walk fifteen meters apart, just the way Chap had been taught at Fort Bragg. Funny, all the anger he'd harbored against Hood and Gonzales was gone. These guys were his family, just like Hood had said that first night at chow. Not necessarily people you'd pick, but people you depended on just the same. The fear, the desire to survive, tied Chap to them with a bond stronger than blood.

As they neared the treeline at the edge of a rice paddy, Hood motioned for the patrol to stop. He directed Gonzales to walk point. Gonzales wielded a machete and cut through the long grass. The rest of them, muddy from humping the paddies, followed and entered the jungle.

Dense plant growth, dark but alive, filled with sounds: creaks, slithers, rustles, and the call of birds. The darkness pressed against Chap, giving him the sensation of wading through its heaviness. The thick overhead canopy bounced above him. Vines caught on his pack and pulled. This bushworld breathed and whispered. It prickled his skin with uncertainty soaking him with fear because even he, and Hood, knew this place was full of booby-traps.

But in this terrible moment, Chap's eyes adjusted. He began to see better here than anywhere else. He could see where each rubber tree leaf ended and the elephant grass began, and he could separate the bamboo stems from that. What had sometimes been a frustrating difference in sight in normal life was a gift from God in this dim, tangled bushworld. Chap's eyes had been made for the jungle.

R.W. was behind Chap. For five long hours they picked their way through the bush. But in all that time, if they'd gone a mile, Chap wouldn't have believed it. When they finally entered a clearing, Gonzales motioned for them to slow down, then sit.

Chap wiped dripping sweat. Slowly he bent his knees and sat on his haunches. The water in his canteen was hot and sickening. The fatigue in his legs made his muscles tremble. It seemed like five hundred mosquitoes were feasting on the back of his neck.

Hood said, "Listen guys, we're less than a hundred fifty meters from the First Platoon."

Stone took off the PRC ("Prick") 25 radio and handed it to Hood. The sergeant made contact with the First. They were elated to know their replacements were near.

"Let's rock and roll," Hood told them.

Stone put the 25 back on his shoulders. He pulled the antenna down in front of his bib and started walking.

Other than the continuous feasting on any patch of exposed skin by the mosquitoes, they had no problems as they made it the rest of the way.

Changing of the guard was uneventful. Chap told R.W., "This ain't so bad, is it?" He knew it was bad, but it felt good to get rid of the 25. R.W.'s face was thick with red welts. Blood streaked his face where he'd scratched. His fatigues were stiff with mud and sweat, and his eyes were pale with exhaustion and fear.

"You're nuts if you don't think we're in some real shit here," R.W. said. "The chaplain back home said this would be the best year of our lives, but . . . he was just full of shit like the rest of them. If this is the best year, then we got nothin' to look forward to if we do make it out of here, and I mean nothin'."

After they ate and rested, Hood gathered them for instructions. "Listen guys, this is it. The LP position is made of four different areas. All we're to do is listen. This trail has been an NVA [North Vietnamese Army] trail. If they come by, we do nothing. We don't even make radio contact until we know our sound can't be heard. Do you understand? This is a wait-and-see thing, not a shoot 'em up."

Stone and R.W. had first watch on the west end. Again, their biggest struggle was trying to keep the mosquitoes from eating them to death. They tied handkerchiefs around their necks to cut down on the welts.

Darkness soaked the landscape, blending with the vegetation. With it came rain, so heavy and forceful it blinded and deafened. It created a wall the mosquitoes could not penetrate. There was no sleep, only long miserable hours of pounding rain.

Finally, morning showed up pale and damp. Replacements arrived. When Hagland and Macabee saw the shape Stone and R.W. were in, they had a good laugh. Bright red welts showed against R.W.'s pale skin. His eyes were swollen from lack of sleep. Neither of them had wanted to foul their position by relieving themselves, so their stomachs were sick and cramping.

"It'll get better, boys," Macabee said. "It'll get better."

Hood's platoon stayed another day and was relieved again by

Second Platoon. On their way back to the base, Hagland was pointman and Gonzales held the map and compass. They were over halfway home when Hagland gave them the hand signal to drop.

Stone couldn't figure out what was going on because he couldn't see ahead. Hood crawled next to Chap and motioned him forward. Together, they reached R.W. and did the same, on up the line.

Progress was painstakingly slow. Finally, Hood crawled all the way forward. Whatever waited in the clearing below, Gonzales had it in his sights, and looked ready to shoot. Hood grabbed Gonzales by the back of his neck. Nose-to-nose, they conferred, quiet but intense. Gonzales relaxed his aim, and Hood released. The sergeant's face was a deep ruddy red when he motioned them forward.

They looked down the small clearing. Not forty feet away Chap saw the thick-muscled yellow fur and dark stripes of a tiger. Chap guessed his weight at near five hundred pounds. Beneath the beast's paws was the body of a black-clad Vietnamese soldier, no larger than an American twelve-year-old boy.

With a deep swipe of his paw, the tiger slit through the skin and muscle of the man's torso from chest to stomach. He took a healthy bite of intestines, twisting his head right and left. The soldier's pink guts tied him to the tiger's red mouth like umbilical cords.

R.W. gagged. Hood put his finger to his lips, shook his head, his eyes telling them don't move, don't talk, don't touch, don't do anything but listen and watch.

The strength of the tiger amazed Stone as he neatly gutted the body. He heard R.W. heave again, and felt his own throat spasm.

Hood looked at Chap, daring him to puke. Chap swallowed hard and willed his stomach to still. With the tiger thoroughly engrossed in his feasting, the sergeant motioned for the men to back off. Slowly, quietly, they eased away on elbows and knees, backtracking a safe distance, then resuming their original trek.

### 

Chap took his first step into a clearing. Hood told them their bunker would one day be heaven. That day had arrived. The humble hole in the ground called to Chap now.

He didn't understand it when Hood whizzed past him and approached Gonzales. He put a hand on Gonzales' shoulder and spun him around. Swiftly, he kicked Gonzales in the privates.

Gonzales went to his knees and then fell on his side. Hood kicked him in the ribs. Gonzales rolled onto his back, his knees still drawn. Hood poked the shotgun in Gonzales's mouth. "If you'd shot that tiger, you'd've given away our position, and got us all killed."

Gonzales panted, hands crossed over his privates. The sight of Hood's gun in his mouth was more horrific than the feasting tiger.

"Can I count on you to never do that again?"

Grimacing, Gonzales nodded.

Hood pulled the gun away and took a step back. "Get up."

Chap looked aside while Gonzales struggled to his feet.

"I'll take point for a while," Hood told Hagland. Hagland picked up the map and compass where they'd flown from Gonzales's grip.

As they started to walk back to Black Horse, Chap fell in with Hood.

"You did good this time out. Even though nothing much happened, you're coming back in one piece," Hood said.

Stone couldn't believe his ears. He'd expected Hood to tell him to fall back, and get the hell away. "Thanks."

"We haven't got too much farther to go."

They walked at a very slow pace. Suddenly, a red parrot shot out of its ground nest directly in front of them. Startled, Hood's gaze followed the parrot. But Chap kept his attention low enough to see a wire stretching like a spider's web before Hood's thigh.

"Freeze, Sergeant," Chap said.

Hood stilled, his gaze following Chap's to the trip wire against his leg. One more step and he'd have set off whatever was attached to the other end.

Chap traced the wire into the foliage. It led to a Falstaff can propped in a tree. A shotgun shell projected from the can's bottom. On top was a small grenade that would kick it into the air and blow it up.

Stone placed a retainer clip from a grenade in the eye of the tripcord. "Okay, man, back off," he told Hood.

Chap tried not to see the fear in Hood's eyes, the terror as he eased his leg from contact with the wire.

When the rest of the patrol caught up, they saw what had happened. "You saved Hood. You saved him, man."

Hood wiped away the sweat on his forehead. He extended his hand for a brief shake of Chap's. "Thanks."

Chap didn't know what to say. He didn't want to explain being colorblind, how he could see things no one else could, how the wire had stood out like a streak of silver light.

### 

That evening, the party began. So did the drinking. Lots of people congratulated the newbie, fresh in, who'd saved Hood's life.

Hood sat by himself and drank alone, no high-jinks, no laughter. Chap abstained, keeping his promise to God. R.W. was already bombed, living it up.

Stone almost preferred the cocky side of Hood to this silent, remote brooder. When the sergeant disappeared, Chap walked to Hood's bunker. He hesitated for a while and then decided to go for it. Quietly, Stone descended the steps. He heard nothing, no movement, not so much as a snore.

Hood sat on his cot in the dim light, his back against the wall. A bottle leaned against his leg. A cup of booze balanced on his knee. "Get out of here," he said.

Something was wrong. Not knowing what to say, Chap turned to go.

"Wait a minute," Hood said.

Chap hesitated. Slowly he turned and faced Hood, standing straight. "Listen," Hood's speech was clear, in spite of the half empty bottle. "You see that shotgun? That shotgun is for close kill. Most don't know that'll kill what you can't see. You guys shoot with the 16. You shoot twenty rounds. I got forty pellets in each shell. I kill before I can hear or see."

Hood sat straighter and looked from the gun to Chap. "I want you to have that, man. You earned that today. You carry it."

Chap's hands hung at his sides. He wet his lips and tried to think of something to say. "I don't deserve this. I didn't do anything. You keep your gun, you'll need it tomorrow."

Hood shook his head. "You earned more than your stripes today, you earned that gun. You got it. Take it, and get the hell out of here."

Chap wiped his sweaty palms against his pant legs. He approached Hood and took the shotgun and a bandoleer of shells. "I don't know what to do with them," he said.

Hood wouldn't look at him again. Chap felt ridiculous, so turned and walked slowly up the stairs with Hood's weapon. Maybe when the sergeant sobered up, he'd want his stuff back. Chap decided to stow it carefully in his bunker until morning.

He'd nearly reached his quarters when the distinctive sound of a .45 split the air. Chap hit the deck like everyone else. Someone hollered, "Medic! Get the medic! Get the medic. It's Hood! It's Hood!"

Doc and the two other medics ran out of their hootch. They entered Hood's bunker and everyone waited outside. In seconds, Doc came out alone.

"Hood's dead," Doc said. "He put a gun in his mouth and killed himself." Doc looked around at the crowd, then he saw Stone, and for a few seconds they stood that way, looking at one another.

# BLACK HORSE, 1969
## ROGER MURPHY
### CHAPTER 4

> "Until a man fulfills his calling, it's like a light only he can see."
>
> —Doc

Ironic that Sergeant Hood would be Doc's first casualty. He helped another medic, Slick, take Hood to be washed and bagged.

Slick was a young black guy just barly eighteen, short, just over five foot five and slightly built. Doc left off filling out Hood's papers and watched Slick's bizarre ritual.

The medic sponged Hood tenderly, his hands dark against Hood's gray skin. "Gotta send him home to mama, nice and clean. Thank you God, this ain't me. Forgive me Lord 'cause you know I'm afraid," Slick prayed aloud like God was resting his elbows somewhere near Hood. "Let Sergeant Hood's soul in the Promised Land, Lord. He done his duty." With long fingers, Slick picked up a joint, kicked back his head and took a deep drag. When he exhaled, the washing resumed. And praying. "Yeah, Sergeant Hood was a righteous soldier."

Doc feared that the sight of Slick washing down Hood would haunt his dreams forever, but he couldn't look away.

When Hood's body was ready, Doc helped Slick zip the bag, put it on the gurney and strap it down. He touched Hood's foot. Only days ago, the sergeant held a gun to an old man's head. He'd pulled the trigger without humanity or justification. Then he'd kicked the corpse, enraged.

Would they meet now, in eternity, the old man and the angry sergeant?

"Oh, God," Doc whispered, "I don't know how to pray. It doesn't make sense. Hood punished himself, and I hope it's enough. Have mercy on him . . . cause if you don't . . . maybe you're just like him with the old man . . . I mean, there has to be some mercy somewhere."

He thought Hood a devil, but how could the devil be zipped in a bag? No, if Hood were the devil, then the war would have stopped the moment he ate a bullet. Hood didn't have any power. None of them did.

"I'll take his body down to the chopper unit," Doc told Slick, watching his thin cheeks pull on the reefer. Slick nodded, his eyes glazed from the weed. He was done now, looking for a high to get him out of here fast.

On the way to the unit, Doc figured he was like a pallbearer, a funeral procession of one for Hood. Man, there was no ceremony, just the facts and the sun came up in the morning, and the bugs were singing their songs and one guy's death didn't mean much, or did it mean everything, every awful thing that could be named?

He watched them load the body on the chopper. It whirred and rose into the sky—Hood's resurrection, the only one Doc feared the sergeant was likely to get.

###

At midday, in the high heat, Doc cut the sleeves off his T-shirt. He didn't dare do the same to his BDU (battle dress uniform) or the sun would cook his skin, but he split the seams of his pant legs to get air. As he crossed the compound in search of Chap, the heatwaves shimmered from the ground. The intense humidity formed on every available surface—leaves, the top of a cab, on the side of a PC or a tank. An egg would fry hard on the top of a five-ton hood.

Doc took a long, warm, and sour drink of Ballantine beer. Another can rode in his pocket. The army must have gotten a deal on this load. It looked and tasted green, but still beat the taste of the water. He went from bunker to bunker asking if anyone had seen Chap.

Of course, no one had. Since they were standing down for a few days and he wasn't on duty, Doc stopped when asked, had a drink, and made small talk, which was big talk, because it was all they had, this world they created in-between times. He'd long since sweated out that first beer when he found Chap at the northwest corner of a bunker. His friend sat, back laid against a pillbox.

The pillboxes were six sandbags wide, dug down about eight to ten feet with concrete and wire mesh on top. They were mostly used for guard duty at night. A man could crawl in the pill box and put up a night scope and machine gun. In the morning, the towers would take over.

Doc climbed fifteen feet to reach Chap. The shotgun from Hood lay across his lap. His hands rose gently up and down the stock. Doc looked at his face, figured the name Stone matched his chin. There was anger in his eyes, frustration in the set of his lips, and desperation in his appearance. His body told you he was in pain.

Beads of sweat covered Chap's forehead, and his clothes were drenched. There wasn't a canteen or beer in sight. Doc wondered if Chap had drank anything today and if he was dehydrated, unable to think straight.

"Hey, newbie. Would you like a beer?"

For the longest time, Stone didn't answer. Doc started to ask again, but Stone cut him off, "Yeah. I'll drink a beer."

Doc didn't know Chap all that well, but had sensed they were alike since that first day. They were green, sure, but Chap had something to him, something unexplainable that connected the two.

"What are you doin' here, man?" Doc plopped beside Stone before handing him the Ballantine.

Back and forth Chap shook his head. He didn't know what he was doing here, in this place. "Why'd he give me the shotgun?

He could've given it to Gonzales." Chap said this like they had been engrossed in a conversation about Hood.

"Now that bastard's going to be our platoon sergeant," Chap continued. "He's nothing but a collector of death. They say he takes souvenirs—belt buckles, pictures, a flag. Some say there was a time he collected ears. I wouldn't doubt it either." Chap took a long drink of the Ballantine. "No telling what he does with that stuff. Bad enough people die in this place without someone like him keeping trophies."

They sat in silence for most of an hour.

"You saved Hood's life," Doc said.

"What good did it do? If he'd've died with that wire . . . that would make more sense. Now I've got this shotgun. What should I do with this shotgun?"

"You can keep it and use it like Hood wanted you to, or put it up and Gonzales will get it. What do you think?"

Chap held the gun away, as though really looking at it for the first time. "I ain't gonna carry it for Hood." He let it rest on his shoulder and drained the beer. "I'll carry it for me. Guess if Hood found rounds for it, I can too."

The air was thick with the smell of excrement being burned in oil drums with diesel fuel. Stone and Doc looked across rows and rows of razor wire. Beyond the wire were the minefields, then more wire, and more mines, and more wire. The jungle had been cut back by bulldozers and plows. What vegetation remained was held back with spray that turned everything orange and black.

It was about a hundred fifty yards all around the perimeter that they had a clear killing zone. But no matter how hard they tried to stay alive, they could never know when the sleeping-creeper death would come.

"If it wasn't for the razor wire, it'd be pretty here," Doc said.

Chap didn't comment.

"Have you seen the duty roster, Chap?"

"No, I haven't seen anything much today."

"You need to go check it. I think you've got guard duty the next couple of days."

###

Doc and Chap went back to the mess tent. Doc had already figured out that if chow was passable, the cook, Rabid, had been straight that day. If chow was bad, he was high. Today was a good day—instant whipped potatoes with gravy, rolled turkey, and water that was distilled with chlorine.

Hood was right. There were two types of soldiers, not good or bad, mean or nice, capable or flunky, black, white, Indian, or Hispanic. Just heads and juicers.

Looking across the mess tent, Doc easily saw the difference. He hadn't touched alcohol before the night of his arrest. Now, he preferred beer over the water, had to admit it brought some relief from the uncertainty, the tragedy. Life was fragile here, so fragile. All they had was the present, a moment you didn't want to feel too much—so pick your way out, Doc thought.

Doc and Chap found seats next to Macabee. "How did Rabid get his handle?" Doc asked.

Macabee cut his turkey into even, bite-sized pieces. "Just watch him when he ain't had no heroin in three days and you'll see why."

Macabee was from South Carolina. He said he was from Charleston, the only place in America where a man learned to be a gentleman. He made no bones about his affluent background, and liked to put on airs. Doc figured if his daddy really had any money, he'd've gotten out of the war.

"Rabid is a real head, I mean stone cold. He's a heroin addict," Macabee said.

"How's he get the stuff?" Chap asked.

"Soda girls at the front gate sell the shit, along with speed and pot and a few special treats. We tried to help Rabid clean up one time, but after the third day he started slobbering like a rabid dog. Hood said to let him kill himself if he wanted to. Long as he can cook, he don't have to fight."

It was getting dark when they came out of the mess tent. Top hollered, "Mail call!"

Stone and Doc passed. Unlike the married guys, or guys with girls back home, they had no reason to dog Top. They opted for the showers instead. In Chap's bunker they undressed, then walked to the Aussie shower each with a towel around his waist. The Aussie allowed a man a gallon of water hanging in a canvas bag. Doc unscrewed the spout, quickly got wet and tightened it down. Chap told Doc about seeing the tiger on patrol while they soaped over welts and sunburn.

Doc had barely rinsed when the water ran out. Chap was just as bad, with soap bubbles still covering half his head.

Macabee, who was just arriving, had a good laugh at their expense. "Not exactly like those nice, hot, hour-long showers back home. And one of these days you boys are gonna figure out that using soap draws mosquitoes."

Chap and Doc hadn't figured that out yet. They were still newbies.

### 

Back at the medic's hootch that evening, they got up a card game. Doc had just been dealt a hand straight from poker heaven when he heard a new sound. Chap had already heard it and was poised with his hands on the edge of the table. Macabee and Sutherland dove to the ground, and the Newbies followed suit.

Their ears exploded and the whole world shook.

Macabee hollered, "Virgin incoming tonight." He got on his feet and swatted the dust off his pants.

A second missile hit, and Macabee dropped, covering his head. The ground shook, again. Again. And again, but farther away.

"Charlie be walking shit across the compound. Give it thirty seconds and the 155s will be cranking it back up. We'll be returning fire for the next hour. Better put your ear plugs in and kick back cause you ain't gonna be gettin' out of here for a while. Hope you ain't gotta shit now, boys."

For the next couple of hours the 155 and 175 millimeter canons returned fire every three to five seconds. The backlash was almost as bad as the incoming. Doc felt the heat from the recoil push across the compound. The noise deafened. How would the canon cockers have their heads intact when this was over? Doc thought.

Doc had heard it said that artillery was so good that, given the right coordinates, they could hit a gnat on the side of a tree at five miles away or farther.

"This ain't nothing new," Macabee said. "Charlie shoots awhile at us, we shoot awhile back. The guys that'll really catch hell tonight are the guys on a bunker."

"When's your first night of guard duty, Stone?"

"Tomorrow night's my first night."

"Well, we'll get with Strickland in the morning, fix your ass up."

Stone said, "Macabee, why do you think Hood did it?"

"I don't know, man. It don't mean nothin'."

"It does mean something. I mean, he was here, he was with us, he was alive yesterday. Why do you think he did it?"

"Listen man, let it go. Here today, gone tomorrow, it don't mean nothin'. All we got is now. It don't mean nothin'."

# BLACK HORSE, VIETNAM, 1969
# CHAP STONE
# CHAPTER 5

> "If you want to know what a man is made of, forget what he says and watch what he does."
>
> —Hatti

Even Vietnam port calls started early. "Get your funky skunky asses up," First Sergeant called. "Rock and roll soldiers, this is not a Holiday Inn. Formation. Get up. Good old PT in the morning."

"PT in the middle of nowhere?" Chap muttered through a Ballantine hangover.

It was for real. Top had been a soldier's soldier all his life. He strode before the ragtag line looking like a poster child for the Army Times. His clothes were immaculately starched and pressed. Shoes high glossed. Hat fit tight around his forehead.

They were sweating, while Top was cool, hollering, "Attention."

Top gave all the information required for the day. "Sergeant Gonzales will be temporarily taking over Hood's position as platoon sergeant. Your new leader is due anyday. In the meantime, you'll be catching the shit details, and staying on the compound until we get things squared away." He looked up and down the line. "Are you all right, soldiers?"

Everyone nodded their heads. Chap heard Macabee's mantra, "It don't mean nothin'."

"Okay. Duty officers, Gonzales pick three. Burn shit detail, six for food service, five for guard duty next five days."

After Top left, Gonzales paraded in front of the platoon, head bobbing, smile fixed and smug. "When in charge . . . take fucking charge."

He let that sink in, strutting like a bantam rooster. "Stone, Strickland, Hatti . . . ," he tapped his lip, looked up and down the line, ". . . what other dumb son of a bitch do I want to put on guard duty for the next five days? R.W. Who else?"

Scavenger. Predator, Chap thought. Everyone hated Gonzales. None of them could do anything about it. Rank had its privilege.

"Get your weapons clean, the 50s and Starlights. Get your stuff together. Dismissed."

The next five days they had guard duty, twelve hours on, twelve off. They could sleep during the day. Five days were a real stretch. Gonzales could have spread the duty around if he wasn't such a bastard.

Hatti was Stone's first guard companion. For the five months he'd been in Nam, Hatti had fought in several skirmishes. The Indian's warm gray eyes didn't miss anything. On at least three patrols he walked point for Hood. Anytime a soldier did that and returned to Black Horse alive, it was a major deal. He was the slickest weapon cleaner Stone had ever seen. He took the 60 apart and put it back together in total darkness. Stone was grateful to have Hatti for a teacher his first time out.

"Where you from, man?" Stone asked as he took apart each clip of the 16 for dust.

"New Mexico."

Chap had learned there wouldn't be more explanation. Knowing his name and state was enough. Nothing personal. The less they knew about one another, the less it hurt to say goodbye.

The first night of inspection, First Sergeant Top stood tall in fatigues and hat with no sweat marks and spit-shined boots. He looked closely at their weapons.

Top smiled, impressed. "You boys be careful. Charlie ain't out there walking around the mortar rounds for no reason. We're expecting some soft touching. There's at least one NVA division coming this way."

Chap nudged Hatti. "How many in one of Charlie's divisions?"

"Around five thousand, just like us."

There might be six to eight hundred men stationed at Black

Horse. Lined up next to five thousand, the odds were dismal. If Chap needed any incentive to stay awake that night, he had it.

It was hot in the bunker. To the right of the slot, Stone saw a ball of gnats that turned out to be mosquitoes. Hatti opened his Marlboros, put one in his mouth and blew smoke. He lit two or three others and stood them on end. Pretty soon the mosquitoes left, but smelling the thick smoke made Stone sick.

Hatti laughed. "It's better than needing a transfusion."

Heavy cloud cover darkened the night. Chap was wired, weighted with responsibility, unable to relax, and scared to death.

"You get first watch, Stone." Hatti pulled something out of his pocket. It was a hammock. "We can't stay awake forever. You take the first watch, I'll take the second."

That's how the night began. Chap felt alone, at the tip of a war he scarcely understood. The darkness fooled his eyes. Sounds were unfamiliar. Mosquitoes whined in his ears. Chap slapped at his cheeks. How long would it be before he could lie snoring in the sling, pretending to be carefree?

At 2335 hours, he woke Hatti. Hatti ran his hand through his hair and stood near Stone, looking out the slot. "Ever look through a Starlight scope?"

"No," Chap said.

"Well, this is your first lesson."

## The Longest Monday

The scope was the size of a large camera lens. They put it on a monopod. The Starlight took moonlight and turned it into daylight. Now Chap could see anything in the kill zone that moved—cat or dog, man or woman.

They took turns looking up and down the perimeter. Everything seemed quiet. At 0325 hrs., the spiral whistling noise of incoming mortar broke the silence. As expected, Charlie walked the incoming every fifteen meters. It hit a fuel tank truck, and color exploded into the air. The 155s cut loose, their percussion shaking the bunker.

Hatti pulled out some plugs and poked them in his ears. He handed a pair to Chap. They covered the plugs with their hands as the 155s pounded and the heat from recoil shook the air.

For fifteen minutes the canon cockers let it go. Chap and Hatti waited for the silence. When it came, the contrast was amazing after being under the tremendous roar of the big guns.

The rest of the first night was uneventful. The second day and night was even more uneventful. The tedium of the third night was worse, with more mosquitoes. Fourth night equally miserable. On the fifth, Chap prayed for strength to finish all three hundred and sixty-five days of his active duty sentence in Vietnam . . . without cracking.

Hatti said he'd take the first watch.

"You got what it takes, Stone."

Considering they hadn't said twenty-five words in the last four days, Chap found this admonition miraculous. "Thanks, man."

### ###

One thing Chap had learned in this longest five days of his life was that he could tell his body when to rest and it listened.

Hatti woke Chap at 0035 hrs. Like the four previous nights, Charlie announced his presence and the canon cockers returned fire.

An hour after they ceased fire, Hatti was lying down, and Chap looked across the killing zone. Something seemed out of place. He grabbed the Starlight scope, put it on the monopod, and looked across the fields. Nothing, but after staring at this same scene day in and out, Chap knew it wasn't right.

He watched for a long, tense fifty minutes. Slowly, a bush moved to the right.

"Hatti."

Hatti rolled out of the hammock. Chap backed from the scope and Hatti looked. He dropped to his knees, picked up the landline, and cranked it twice.

"We got movement at the exit perimeter wire."

Chap quickly let go of a hand flare, but they could see nothing. They kept watching and waiting, but nothing moved.

At 0415 hrs., they still watched. Hatti had not left Chap's side. Fear pried their eyes open wide. Hatti had the Starlight scope. Chap simply watched. Then they spied it again, movement. Not just one bush this time, but at least ten.

Chap hollered, "Probe in the wire." They kicked off a flare. Chap put the 60 to his shoulder and let it rip. The red tracer rounds scattered dust in the kill zone. Hatti grabbed the M79, kicked off a grenade, then two, then three.

Over the landline came Top's voice, "What the hell are you firing at?"

"We've got movement out here, near the wire," Hatti said, describing what they'd seen.

Top didn't believe them. Again things quieted down. They watched and waited.

Sunrise came, and with it a view of the wire. They called Top on the landline. "Get down here, now."

Chap and Hatti were quiet while they waited for Top's arrival. When he came, he viewed the wire through binoculars. "Damn, I don't believe what I'm seeing. There's something out there, on the wire."

Top got the map showing them the location of each land mine. They walked to the end of the killing zone, the place where the razor wire began. Chap's stomach ached every time the ball of his foot touched the ground. He wanted to run ahead, see what or who hung on the wire. Stone wanted to run away, all the way home, be done with this war.

Charlie had gotten through the first section of wire. Hanging at the crosswires were two bodies. Their swollen bellies showed them as pregnant women. Nothing above the breast line remained, on either one.

Hatti whistled through his teeth, a deflating sound. "An insight into the soul of our enemy. People who send their most valuable possession into a war to die intend to win the son of a bitch?"

These people were not dumb gooks, as Chap had been told in basic and Advanced Training. Charlie was a ruthless soldier that would go to any lengths to win. One death, two deaths of innocent victims meant nothing with a war to win.

Chap couldn't pull his eyes away from the headless women. He'd killed them with the 60. Women, pregnant women.

"Don't bring anything home you can't give to me," his mother whispered.

He hadn't wanted this—this war, this, Vietnam. What was Mom doing now, right now on the other side of the world? Was she baking a pie, watering her violets, staring at the woodline thinking proud thoughts of him?

Charlie was a woman, Charlie was a woman with a baby in her stomach. Two women, two babies. The U. S. Army hadn't told him that, not in weapons training, not during cadence or the bullshit speeches at the end of training.

If he was going home alive, he'd have to be just as ruthless, just as bottomline as Charlie.

Standing next to Top and Hatti, he made his choice. He was going home alive. What he had to do, he'd do. But he was going home. A new monster entered him then.

# CHAP STONE
# VIETNAM, 1969
# CHAPTER 6

> "Hard times may or may not make a man strong, but they sure as hell reveal where he's weak."
>
> —Chap Stone

Stone rolled over in his cot underneath the light poncho liner and rubbed the mosquito bites on his arms. It felt like his head was going to explode, as if somebody put it in a vise and screwed down tight. He didn't think he'd ever get used to waking with a hangover.

The heat lay over his face like a sheet. He lacked the initiative to puke, but knew with scant effort he could exorcise last night's C-rations all over the bunker.

Yet, this heaviness was more than heat and nausea. A vision of dead, headless women filled his thoughts. They came to him in his dreams, told his mother, and she cried while he'd tried to explain, until he had to shoot them again, and again.

Chap had just pulled on one jungle boot and begun to tighten the laces when a runner came to the door. "Top wants your ass now, baby killer."

The runner left before Chap could react. "Baby killer." He

stood and looked around for something to smash. How could they call me that? He didn't choose for those women to come across that wire. He didn't choose for them to put twenty-five pounds of C4 explosives on their backs.

Chap jammed his left foot into his boot. That better be the last time someone called him baby killer—the very last.

With brisk, angry movements Chap brushed his fatigue jacket. He shoved his arms in the sleeves, rolling them to show his rank. Snatching his jungle hat and cramming it onto his head, he came out of the ground.

Daylight hit him in the face, warm on his cheeks. Chap breathed deep, sought peace, a release from his anger, but couldn't find it. He grabbed his shotgun and headed to the Command Post (CP) hootch.

### 

In the CP bunker, Chap returned Top's salute. "PFC Stone reports as ordered, First Sergeant."

"At ease. Sit down, soldier."

Top seemed different than usual, more relaxed. This made Chap nervous.

"Captain wants to see you, but before he does I want to tell you, son, I'm proud of you."

For a second, Chap felt his guts tighten in a knot that made it hard to breathe.

Top told him again, "You did your job, Stone, and I commend you for it."

The old soldier's words gave Chap some ammo against the hated name "baby killer," against the great black hole which had opened deep inside. He wanted to cry, but he was too sick and angry. He wanted Top to reassure him again, and again. The job was beyond him, beyond anything he'd ever heard of. But if they were pleased, if they thought it was right for him to kill pregnant women, then he wasn't the man for this Army.

Top went to the captain's side of the bunker and quickly returned. "The captain will see you now."

Like First Sergeant, the captain spoke to Chap like he was a hero. "It's not often that I say thanks. You ensured the safety of the compound and didn't let those bodies get off the wire. We turned those bodies over to the ARVNs (Army of the Republic of South Vietnam) this morning and told the battalion. It looks good for us.

"I know that you had an unusually long five-day stretch. Sergeant Gonzales probably had a good reason for that, and it was apparently successful. I'd like to help you enjoy life for a day. You can ride the mail truck in and stop off for a cold one wherever you guys like to do that. When the truck comes back from Long Ben, I'll have them pick you up. Understand me, soldier?"

Chap struggled to shift. He'd been a newbie, then a lifesaver, then his mind had been blown over Hood's suicide, then he'd spent five days in a hot-box and killed two pregnant women, and now, now he was a hero again, and they were giving him a big party. Maybe Macabee was right. Nothing mattered. Nothing at all mattered.

"I understand, Sir. Anything else, Sir?"

"That will be all."

"One additional request, Sir. Specialist Hatti was with me in the bunker, Sir. He pulled the same duty I did, Sir. Is it possible he would be able to come with me, Sir?" Chap knew Hatti was almost as bewildered as he was over the women on the wire.

"Specialist Hatti, Sergeant Gonzales, and yourself may go, soldier."

###

Stone wasn't going to let Gonzales ruin his day off. Top told him to tell the men they had twenty minutes to get on the truck.

Chap got Hatti just rolling out of his cot. "We get to report to the mail truck and ride as escorts to Long Ben. Captain says we can stop off along the way and have a cold one."

Hatti belted an Indian war cry right out of a John Wayne western. "We'll have us a time today."

His enthusiasm made Chap smile as he hurried to his own bunker and donned the cleanest clothes he had. He did some quick housekeeping and grabbed the dirty stuff to take to the housegirls at the gate for a washing.

The three of them reached the five-quarter at the same time. Gonzales crowded in front with the driver, while Hatti and Stone climbed in back. There were two bench seats that would hold four to six guys, or fold up when not in use. Down the middle of the bed was a bar, four and one-half inches around and chest high. An M60 machine gun with butterfly handles rode on top of it, with a box of two hundred rounds, and a bandoleer of shells. With the butterflies, the M60 could be held like a pistol with two hands. Looking down its barrel wasn't as accurate as putting a stock to your shoulder, but one glimpse of such a mean gun and the thought of its hellacious fire would intimidate anyone.

It was hot in the truck. Stone leaned forward to see what was taking so long. The young driver was putting on a pair of driving gloves, one finger at a time.

Gonzales was already muttering in Spanish, agitated. It didn't take much to set him off. "Forget those damn gloves and move this truck, man. I'm sweating like a damn hog over here," Gonzales said.

Perturbed, the driver looked at Gonzales and then commenced pulling each finger on his gloves down tight.

Gonzales reached over and slapped the boy, knocking his head to the left. He grabbed the kid by the collar and slapped him again, and once more. The kid whimpered as he raised a gloved hand to his nose and viewed the blood on his leather fingers. "You get your ass goin'," he told the kid, "or I'll cut out your liver and feed it to Charlie."

The kid kicked off the engine and they started down the road.

### 

Black Horse wasn't far off the map at QL 1. In no time, they were on their way to Long Ben. Three-fourths of the way was a little town in Ten Province called Xuan Loc. The driver stopped at the edge of town.

"You're here at 1600 hours sharp. If you're not, I'll leave, and you'll find your own way back to Black Horse and answer to the old man."

Stone spoke before Gonzales could. "Don't worry, man, if we ain't here, you got our permission to leave."

The kid reached up and touched his bruised cheek. "I hope to hell you're not here."

He sped away, dusting up a few rocks. Gonzales ran after, kicking the door of the five-quarter. "Little shit," he called after. "Tryin' to piss me off. Next time I see him, I'm gonna cut his throat."

Hatti put his arm around the sergeant's neck. "Gotta save some of that piss n' vinegar for the ladies, Sarge."

They had a good laugh then. Almost immediately a man pulled alongside in a Lambretta—a little Honda 50 motorcycle with a covered carrier on back for hauling six or seven people.

"How much we go?" Hatti asked the driver.

"Hundred piasta."

That was fifteen or twenty cents back home.

They paid the driver and piled on, while Hatti did another war cry.

It was only 0825 hrs., when they entered Xuan Loc. Up and down the dirt road, little Lambrettas scooted about. Several GIs were on the street, some falling down drunk. There was no way of telling if they'd started early or were still ending up a binge from the day before.

Stone counted fourteen establishments advertising the coldest beer and the hottest women. The women filled doorways. Hard to believe he'd thought them ugly when he'd first come to Vietnam. Now, in their deeply colored silks, with their tiny waists and small round hips, their long black hair, as silky as their garments, Stone had never seen anything so beautiful. Some of their dresses, deep purple, and yellow, or rich sooty black, were slit all the way to their hips, revealing curvy legs and creamy thighs.

They smiled warmly, invitingly. Seeing them, Stone swallowed so loudly he startled himself. Hatti and Gonzales had been observing him.

"Sheee-it," Gonzales muttered before taking a drag of his cigarette.

But Hatti looked ready to burst with laughter. "What you looking at, Stone?"

He didn't want to answer in front of Gonzales. "I'm thinking these ladies ain't so bad looking."

Hatti guffawed. "You ain't seen nothin' yet."

Gonzales told the driver to stop, and they jumped out at a place called Dung Lai—The Stop.

"Know why they call it that?" Hatti asked Stone.

"No."

He slung an arm around Stone's shoulders. "Cause once you walk through those doors, friend, you might never want to come back out."

No other customers were in the Dung Lai, just the proprietor and the women—all extremely beautiful, hair long and black, faces artfully painted with darkly arched brows and red lips, flowing dresses and pants; sensuous, mysterious.

They hadn't walked two steps into the bar when one girl grabbed each of the guys, each saying the same words, "You number one, GI. Buy me drink?"

Before Stone could say yes, Hatti nudged him: "You never buy them a drink, because all they get is tea. You drink first and then they can have a drink."

Disappointed, Chap's girl said, "Oh, GI, you number ten

thousand. We would never do that. We're here to help you. You have a very good time, be number one. I number one girl, you number ten thousand. Oh, GI."

Gonzales was already sitting at a table, a girl on his lap, another draped over his shoulders. Stone and Hatti followed in his wake and sat down.

One of the girls approached to take their orders. "We have Falstaff, Black Label, Ballyhigh, whiskey, Ba-Ma-Ba."

The strange name, Ba-Ma-Ba, caught Stone's attention. "What is that?"

Hatti leaned toward Stone. "You don't know what Ba-Ma-Ba is?"

"No, man. I'm new in country. Take care of me."

"Sheee-it, give us a round of the gook beer," Gonzales said, right before he nibbled on a girl's ear.

"Let me educate you," Hatti said. "Most beers run five percent alcohol. The ones on the base are two point five. Ba-Ma-Ba is gook beer. It runs fifteen percent, does strange things to your brain. They put embalming fluid in the shit."

The young serving girl brought them tall glasses of Ba-Ma-Ba. It was very cold. The first cold drinks they'd had in a while. She set her tray aside and crawled into Stone's lap, wiggling her small behind against his privates. Stone responded immediately, further shocked when her tiny hand covered the source of his response.

"You number one," she purred in his ear.

Hatti fell sideways with laughter. "Look how red your face is, man."

Chap's only place to hide was in his glass. He took a big drink of the beer and nearly gagged on its ugly taste.

The girl's hand rested between his legs, caressing him. He tried to take it in stride, like Gonzales, and look relaxed, like Hatti. Hatti kept laughing, too loud, too often, knowing he wasn't fooling anyone.

The young lady wrapped her arm around Stone's neck, pressed soft lips along the side of his neck. The more she kissed him, the more laughter from Hatti and disgust from Gonzales he inspired.

Two more girls joined them. After the third Ba-Ma-Ba Stone finally had the nerve to ask the girl her name.

"Lyn. I make beaucoup love to you. I make very good love to GI."

Stone thought for a second. "Beaucoup love me? You only just met me."

"I beaucoup love you for only twenty dollars."

"Twenty dollars?"

Hatti spit beer all over when Stone finally figured out the girl was a whore. Chap felt like a dumb country bumpkin.

Back in Neosho there were only two whores, both ugly and

used up, neither charging a dime for their favors, or so the story went. Regular girls didn't look you in the eye like this and barter their virtue.

But it wasn't such a bad deal. Twenty dollars? He had more than that, and reached in his pocket to prove it.

"Don't you even think about it," Hatti warned.

"She ain't worth no twenty dollars," Gonzales said, looking the girl in the eye. "You never take first price, man."

Hatti nodded agreement, and Stone shoved the scrip money deep in his back pocket.

Someone put a couple of dimes in the jukebox. The song "American Woman" by the Who came on. The girls got up and started dancing with each other, moving their hips, shaking their breasts.

Another round of beer appeared. The men drank while the song finished. Lyn returned with two of the other girls. They bargained the price for a while. Pretty soon Hatti whispered something in a girl's ear and she got up and left. Hatti gave Stone a thumbs-up sign. "I'll be back." Hattie got up and disappeared in a hallway at the back of the bar.

Gonzales continued to drink, heavily, while Stone watched. In minutes, Hatti returned, smiling. The girl sat behind him, rubbing his chest. "You number one lover," she told him. "The best."

Hatti looked like he believed it. He whispered again in the girl's ear and she giggled. Hatti whispered to Gonzales, and he laughed too.

Stone asked, "What's going on? What's so funny?"

The secret spread. Pretty soon, all the girls crowded around Stone.

"What'd you tell them, Hatti? What's going on?"

Hatti leaned close, "Listen, man, we're trying to take care of you. We're buddies. We care about you. You're new around here. We told the girls you're a cherry boy. They'll give it to you for nothing."

Stone didn't know whether to be angry or elated. "You mean I get it for free?"

"They think a cherry boy's good luck. You'll get it for nothing."

Four of the girls vied for a seat next to Stone. "You cherry boy?" one asked.

Chap didn't even have to act the part. He blushed like a new bride. The girls giggled. One girl got on her knees beside him, laid her head on his lap, rubbed his leg. "We want to make love to you very bad. Who you want? Buddha will be good to us if we make love to you."

Stone's mind was clouded after four or five beers. He was even thinking less when the beautiful ladies rubbed his legs and told him he was wonderful, all the while offering themselves.

It was afternoon when Stone got up. It wasn't Lyn who decided to make love to the cherry boy, but a young girl named Soou Ling. She pulled Stone onto his feet and they made their way around tables, to the back rooms.

Stone straddled a fence between drunk and sober, but he knew full well what he was about to do. Maybe when he was an old man, sixty-five or so, this would come back to him. "This" was now.

Soou Ling had the longest black hair he'd ever seen on a woman. It went all the way down to the curve of her waist. She smelled very differently than American women—musky, but feminine and sweet. She wore no eye makeup, but was still very pretty.

Stone had no idea how old she was. It was hard to make out the age of Vietnamese women. They looked old at twelve, ancient and sun-baked at thirty.

Stone didn't care. At the moment, her age didn't matter.

They entered a very small room, lit by a single dim bulb hanging from the ceiling on a long cord. There was a cot, a small pillow, no cover, and a pan of water on the floor.

Obviously, the room had one purpose. The cot was narrow, barely wide enough to hold Stone's shoulders, let alone two bodies.

Soou Ling stood before him, unbuttoned his fatigue shirt. Often, she looked into his eyes, shy yet eager, as virginal as he was, as efficient as a whore. Ladylike, she dropped to her knees. The backs of her knuckles were warm against his stomach as she undid his belt.

Shaken, Stone took her by the shoulders and pulled her to her feet.

"I'll do that myself. I need to take my boots off first."

She nodded. With one graceful movement Soou Ling crossed her arms and grabbed the hem of her dress, whisking it over her head.

She wore no underclothes. It was the first time Stone had ever seen a woman naked in the flesh. Her breasts were small, perfectly balanced; her nipples dusky, beautiful above her stomach flat.

In the fifteen watts of swinging bulb, she was like a painting, her dark hair slashing its bold straight lines over the fragile pale curve of her shoulder. He followed the curve down her arm to the turn of her waist, to the juncture of thighs, and the faint hairline.

Stone breathed so deeply that Soou Ling laughed, seeming flattered and delighted. "I'll be very good to you, cherry boy."

She rose on tiptoe and kissed him, then laid down and opened her arms.

With leaden movements Stone ripped his boot laces wide, kicked free of his remaining clothes. He approached her, feeling every inch of his six feet body, wondering if he'd hurt her, remembering she'd done this before.

She touched him, guided him, and their breath mingled, making them close. Soou Ling was soft and warm, fragrant and tender. He felt clumsy, and wonderful, desperate with need.

It didn't last very long.

But Chap catalogued it deep inside—the way it felt at that supreme moment when their souls connected. The way, for a second, he felt safe, happy, joyful . . . in a place that inspired none of those things.

###

When Stone came out of the room, Hatti hooted and laughed, drunker than ever. "Was it fast, was it slow, was he good, was he bad?"

Even Gonzales joined in, rapping a heavy beat on the table.

The other girls gathered around Soou Ling and wanted a hug to receive some of the joy that Buddha would give. Stone ordered another beer. The cherry boy had done his manly duty.

As the afternoon waned, Gonzales grew quiet, morose, and brooding, while Hatti, the man of few words, laughed and laughed at absolutely nothing. If they were going to meet the truck at four, Chap needed to shut down his drinking.

Gonzales decided he needed another go in the back room. This would be three, and Chap was impressed.

"You guys go on, do what you want. I'll be road-dog," Chap said.

Gonzales finished his beer. "Road-dog," he sneered. "Don't be doggin' my ass, Stone, if you know what's good for you."

Chap let it go. He wasn't going to fight with the sergeant. Especially when he was too drunk to stand straight.

Soou Ling came over and sat beside Stone. He wrapped his arm around her, kissed her forehead.

She giggled. "You buy me drink now?"

This time he did.

Soou Ling's drink had just been delivered when a piercing female scream came from one of the rooms.

The girls looked at each other, alarmed and afraid. The proprietor marched to the back and beat on the door, shouting in Vietnamese, "Choi oi. Dung lai. Dung lai."

Gonzales cracked the door and slurred, "Get your gook ass back behind the bar. I ain't killing the bitch, I'm taking care of her."

Sputtering in high-pitched Vietnamese, the bartender hurried to Chap's table. "I don't understand you," Chap said.

The man grabbed Chap's arm, urging him to interfere and deal with Gonzales.

It would be no small task to get the sergeant peacefully back to Black Horse. Chap was reluctant to try, to let Gonzales ruin his day after all. He chewed the inside of his cheek while trying to figure out what to do. There'd be no help from Hatti. He was facedown on the table.

Stone got out of his chair and walked toward the room. He couldn't hear anything, and turned back toward the table.

The woman screamed again, and the proprietor got hysterical.

"Calm down," Stone yelled at the man. He reached the door.

On the other side of the door, a woman sobbed and begged in English and Vietnamese.

He pounded his fist against the thin wood. "Gonzales, what's going on?"

The woman screamed and sobbed desperately.

"Gonzales, open the door, man."

The door whipped open. "You doggin' me, man?" Gonzales drew his chin down as he wobbled unsteadily.

"Listen, SargE, come on out. We gotta go. The MPs will be here in a minute."

For five or six tense seconds, Gonzales blocked the doorway.

"Leave the bitch alone, man," Chap spoke as calmly as he could. "She ain't worth the trouble if those MPs come."

Gonzales staggered into the hall, one boot on, one arm in his shirt, pants undone.

Chap pushed around him and looked at the girl. She sat huddled on the cot. Her face looked like it'd been shoved through a windshield. Violet bruises were already raised on her swollen cheeks.

Chap wanted to kill Gonzales.

Gonzales was so drunk, he couldn't even fit the brass tip of his belt through his military buckle.

Stone grabbed both ends of the belt. It was all he could do to touch Sergeant "Speedy" without putting a gun to his head and pulling the trigger. Gonzales fell against the wall and slid to the floor. Hatti had come to again, waking up and laughing. If the MPs did come in, they'd all be up a creek.

Stone jammed Gonzales's arm into the shirt. "Stand up, man." With a hard yank, he got the sergeant on his feet, leaned his bulk against a wall, and held him there while he checked his watch. Almost three. Thanks to Gonzales, that kid would enjoy leaving them stranded.

"Leave my ass alone," Gonzales muttered. "Get away."

He heaved and started puking. Stone backed away, in time to save his boots. The sergeant barreled between tables, upended chairs, landed hard against the bar, puking all the way.

"Dung Lai!" the bartender hollered. "Dung Lai!"

But Gonzales didn't stop.

Chap went outside and hailed a Lambretta. It came quickly. He hustled Hatti and Gonzales outside to the taxi. Hatti was agreeable to getting on first. He lay on his side, still laughing. Gonzales passed out in the doorway. Stone put him in a fireman's carry and heaved him into the back of the Lambretta, letting his boots drag the ground.

A couple of guys from an engineer's battalion stopped by and started laughing. They quit laughing when the proprietor came out with a machete, ready to hack Gonzales to bits for ruining his whore. "Caca Dav!" he screamed.

One engineer grabbed the man's arm and broke the blade

against the side of the building. With the exception of Soou Ling, the girls came out to scream and kick at Gonzales.

Chap tried to calm everyone down. He shoved Gonzales's feet onto the bed of the taxi and went through his pockets, finding twenty-two dollars of MPC (military payment certificate) money. Hurrying, he entered the bar and gave this to the proprietor to help make restitution for the sergeant's unholy deeds. He then fled Dung Lai with a chorus of heated Vietnamese at his back.

### 

They made it to the pickup point in adequate time. The taxi driver even helped Stone pull Gonzales off the platform. Hatti could still function, but he tried to fight the driver. "No good gooks. All the gooks should be dead."

"What the hell is wrong with you people?" Stone said to Hatti as he restrained him. "This was supposed to be a good time. Damn it."

For fifteen minutes Chap watched for the truck. Gonzales was still out cold, and Hatti had his head between his legs. Finally, Chap heard the drone of the approaching vehicle.

The driver didn't look any happier than when he'd dropped them off. "We need to leave that son of a bitch lying right where he is," he told Chap, motioning toward Gonzales.

"No we don't, man. He'd have your ass for supper."

"Look at my face. Look at what that bastard did to my face."

Stone dragged Gonzales's carcass toward the truck. "You ought to see what he did to this girl's face at the bar."

Hatti said, "I can't find my face."

The back of the five-quarter was stuffed with mail bags. Stone hoisted Gonzales on top of the bags. Hatti climbed in on his own.

"I'm riding up front. Had enough of you two." No sooner had Chap taken his seat than he turned to see Hatti holding the butterfly handles of the M60. "That's the last place I want to find you, behind a gun."

Stone climbed in the back and pushed Hatti onto his butt. Then he tapped the driver on the shoulder. "Let's head for the house."

It was less than twenty miles to Black Horse. They were going only twenty-five miles per hour. It was a safe trip, but a trip that aged Stone. Things had gotten out of hand. The thought of Soou Ling invaded his mind, ruined by the vision of Gonzales's whore, looking bludgeoned by a tree.

Less than a mile to Black Horse, there was a little village. In front of its entrance, two headless bodies hung upside down on crosses.

"We gave the bodies to the ARVNs," Chap remembered Collins saying.

As the truck drew closer, then abreast, Chap caught sight of a small hand, visible through one of the stomach wounds, reaching beyond the blood, for the light, for the air.

"Baby killer."

He heard it again, said only this morning. It didn't matter what Sergeant Right said, what Captain Collins said, it was the truth. Connected to the small hand was a small life. He, Chap Stone, his mother's son, had snuffed it out and he knew he'd see those small fingers for the rest of his life.

Everything he'd been drinking this long day burned its way up his throat. He lost the "gook beer" on the mailbags, on Gonzales, on Hatti, out the back of the five-quarter.

But he couldn't purge himself of the certainty, the assurance . . . Baby killer.

### 

At Black Horse, Chap unloaded Hatti and Gonzales. He went in search of Doc, and a drink, something to take away the foul taste, to soften the barbed edges of truth.

Doc was in the medic's hootch. It was cool there, and they each had a beer. Chap felt himself grab hold of the edge of sanity while Doc told him the events of the day. He had no idea what Doc said, but just listened to the steady tone of his voice, trying to find a footing in the shale.

"There was a girl, back at Xuan Loc. Her name's Soou Ling." He told Doc how it was, nearly all of it. Then he told him about Gonzales, how he'd beat the whore. Chap didn't mention the headless bodies, or the baby's hand. He couldn't.

Doc tapped his beer can against Chap's. "You know, you're a pretty good guy."

Stone smiled. "Now why would Doc say that? "Thanks."

"No reason to thank me. Seemed like it was meant to be from the first. I'm thinking we're a lot alike."

Stone took a long drink. "Don't sell yourself short, buddy. You're not anything like me."

# BLACK HORSE, VIETNAM, 1969
## CHAP STONE
## CHAPTER 7

> "I always thanked God for my mom, her raising me by the golden rule, but here, in the Nam, it's the things the old man taught me about hunting that keep my ass alive."
>
> —Chap Stone

Being from southwestern Missouri, Stone had been in lots of different kinds of weather—thunderstorms, hailstorms, and a god-awful amount of tornadoes. But the Vietnamese monsoon was in a class by itself.

In high school he'd read about monsoons, how they'd dump three to six hundred inches of rain in four or five months. But reading about them was nothing like experiencing their power.

Sticking his arm into the rain was like poking it through silver strands of a curtain. Buckets and tubs of water poured from the sky, cloaking objects around him, bringing darkness to day, and music to his nightmares.

Water pounded the ground like the feet of a marching buffalo herd, a consuming sound that churned a man's insides, threatening to return him to the clay he came from.

The rest of the platoon stomped around in the mud, angry and disgusted. Each hated being in this godforsaken place. They punished themselves up drinking or smoking dope. But Stone grew thoughtful. How powerful God must be to make rain like this. This was a time to recharge life . . . before all hell broke loose, before they could kill again, or be killed.

Routine wrapped Stone with its mind-numbing sanctity. He cleaned weapons, pulled guard duty, ate, took the occasional crap, survived malaria pills, tried not to think about all he'd seen during the last weeks of ambush, while letting the rain tamp the memories deep, deep inside.

With the tedium came angry outbursts, quick fights over nothing, and frustration. From all appearances, they hated one another, yet, when the fighting began, they worked as a unit, one life readily laid down for another. That was the irony.

Getting the coveted duty outside of Black Horse helped. Stone lucked out a few times, going on a mail run or pulling security duty outside the gate.

He came in contact with the children wandering the streets then. They amazed him with their soft skin that defied the torturous weather. They were tough, mentally and physically. Yet, they were children, gathering around, smiles bright, thin arms outstretched for chocolate bars, wanting to be liked.

Every day, the detail took certain mama-sans inside the perimeter to wash and clean clothes for the soldiers. The MPs would shake down everything the mamas carried, checking for bombs and weapons. A little old lady shouldn't be capable of hurting anyone, but Stone knew better. In Vietnam, the face of death was male and female, smooth or wrinkled, or pregnant.

When the rain gave reprieve and quiet for a while, the heat rose from the ground, damp and suffocating. Stone's feet were always wet, in spite of the jungle boots. He wondered if he'd ever be dry again. The skin on the bottoms of his feet grew soft and if he scratched them, they bled.

In spite of the hostile landscape, the simplicity and ingeniousness of the Vietnamese people was winning his admiration. Everything had a purpose in Nam, nothing was thrown away, but was recycled and used again. An old battery from a radio had enough spark to set off a land mine. Discarded oil barrels held rice, or laundry, or ammunition. And though these people could smile at you by day and shoot at you by night, Chap had to give them their due.

But he was homesick like everyone else. Ofttimes, the GIs listened to the Armed Forces Radio Network Armed Forces Viet Nam (AFVN) or its competition, Hanoi Hilton, a propaganda station Charlie ran three hours a day. They liked the Hanoi station because it played the best music. But the AFVN station made them feel most connected to the world—the USA. Nam was just a stopover place where death knocked at your door twenty-four hours a day. The States were the real world.

They heard about students protesting the war on college campuses all across America. "What the hell is wrong with those guys, man? Don't they know we're here for them? This is where we're supposed to be. The President sent us."

That was the usual response. When they were drunk, they were more philosophical, and tried to figure out the lack of support from home. Stone took part in the discussions, voicing his disdain like everyone else. When it got too noisy, too out of hand, he'd remember there was only one thing of importance, one thing to keep his attention centered on—completing three hundred sixty-five days alive.

### ###

July 3rd, they received a new platoon leader. Lieutenant Ernson was infantry, and had transferred from a Mac Vee unit which had been attached with ARVNs. Ernson was from Indiana. One by one he asked them, "You play football?"

Some of the boys had played in high school. When they got to Stone he said, "My school was so small we didn't have a team." The rest of the guys laughed and called him a hillbilly.

Ernson walked back to his bunker and returned with a football that they tossed back and forth. "Would you guys be up for a game against the officers, tomorrow on the forth of July? We'll have a hell of a contest."

Gonzales spoke up, "Do we get thrown in the brig if we stomp your asses?"

Ernson laughed. "Not hardly. Touch or tackle's the next question, and there's only one rule for that. It's got to be tackle."

That night, the platoon celebrated their chance to whip the officers.

"Don't get too drunk, gentlemen," Ernson warned. "You're going to need every bit of your strength when we kick your asses tomorrow."

Everyone laughed. They seemed more like a fraternity than a platoon of fighting men.

###

The monsoon came early that fourth of July. They couldn't see fifteen yards in front of them, but Ernson didn't seem to notice the downpouring rain. "Ready to play?"

Yes, they were ready. Lieutenants and captains for the entire battalion met in the middle of the yard. The officers were one team, Stone's platoon was the other. Everyone else was restricted to the sidelines to root and cheer.

Playing all afternoon, the Wolfhounds played hard and laughed hard. Ernson could throw a pass like a bullet. Stone's group didn't find out until later that he'd played for Notre Dame. In the end they were whipped severely. It was one of the best days of the year.

Everyone got drunker than three hundred goats, but Ernson brought something special to the men and Stone appreciated that. He didn't know where Ernson was going to lead them but actually anticipated liking the idea of being under his command.

###

Six days later, Lieutenant Ernson asked for volunteers. "Has anyone escorted convoy vehicles?"

Macabee raised his hand. "When I first got in country seven months ago, I did convoy duty."

"We're going to Long Ben to escort vehicles to another destination. We'll be gone a week to ten days."

Stone volunteered. Long Ben sounded like paradise—hot showers, clean clothes, and new scenery. When their chopper landed on base, the Quonset hut looked like the entrance to heaven.

The group showered for thirty minutes, enjoying the slick feel of soap, lather, clean smells, warmth, and coolness—the entire experience of being clean.

They received a fresh issue of clothes and boots, and a place to sleep. Stone didn't turn his weapon into the armory, but lay the 97 across the foot of his bed, primed and ready, covered with a rolled poncho liner. The 97 was a friend, one Stone wanted close.

When they went to the noncommissioned officer (NCO) recreation hall to have a beer, the military newspaper *Stars and Stripes* lay on one of the tables. Next to it was the *New York Times*. On the front page was a picture of a student burning his draft card.

"What's the matter with these people?" Stone held the picture so everyone could see.

"Must be Communist mothers," Macabee said.

"They need to be here," Sutherland added.

French Fry smacked the picture with his knuckles. "Cowards."

Their response to Stone's question divided them from the rest of the world, more radically than the miles of ocean they'd crossed to get here.

###

The following morning, they were dressed at five. Lieutenant Ernson said they'd be leaving in an hour. At six, a transportation company picked them up for extra security. The convoy was a mile of five- and ten-ton dump trucks with comex boxes on their backs. Stone had no idea what was in those boxes.

Some of the trucks were armed with M60s. That's where the infantry would ride, in the back of the dump truck. This would be gravy duty. They'd be dry and on their butts instead of their boots.

At 0800 hrs. they were still sitting, growing hot and restless. At 0830 hrs., the soda girls came by and Stone had a couple of drinks. At

0900 hrs., transportation contacted Ernson by radio and asked if he was ready to rock and roll.

"We've been ready all morning."

They were headed for a place called Tan In, to reinforce supplies to the twenty-fifth division unit.

The engines roared to life, loud without mufflers, puffing smoke. The convoy moved down the road like a giant accordion, each truck trying to stay close to the one in front, until the diesel fumes grew so thick they'd ease off to breathe. Ernson sat directly behind Stone.

They'd been on the road a couple of hours when the lieutenant received a radio message from the Huey helicopter providing air cover. "We've seen movement up the road a few miles. Proceed with caution."

Immediately Stone leaned close to the windshield; a sense of dread came over him. A whiff of smoke left a rocket-propelled grenade (RPG) to his right. Its trail arrowed into the side of a gas tank two trucks ahead. The five-ton exploded. White, pillar-shaped smoke rose high.

Debris flew through the smoke before the debilitated truck lifted then flipping onto its side. Men screamed from inside the vehicle. The force of the hit must have twisted their bodies.

Stone's driver whipped to the right going to the ditch. Before they stopped, Stone had the door open, taking six steps on the ground, waiting for the distinctive cracks of three that would follow from the AK 47, announcing Charlie's location.

Every vehicle had stopped. The ambush blocked the road. Ernson got on the radio. "Do you see any movement?"

"Negative," the chopper pilot answered.

Ernson threw a small piece of stone. It hit Gonzales on the leg. Ernson gave him the hand signal to gather the troops and get the squad together. He gave the hand signal to move to the right.

They kept a far distance apart and began a search and seizure of the area.

Stone hated the uncertainty. Charlie could have them in his sights, and they wouldn't know. His limbs felt heavy, like they had a mind of their own—like they wanted to run in the other direction. He willed the fear down to his gut. Plodding forward, he watched for Charlie's sign.

Ernson got Stone's attention. He signaled—take left point. Stone nodded and took position, before entering the jungle.

It was better here, and Stone knew he was the only man in the squad who felt that way. But here, he could look for the silver, the strange pewter color that only he could see, telling him a reed had been cut, a leaf turned.

He walked quietly, the way his dad, the Choctaw taught him. When everyone else took three paces, Stone took one, searching the ground for noiseless faces. He listened between his own breaths and watched the shadows.

It took a long time to make a one-eighty sweep. They found the empty canister of the RPG, but didn't see anything human.

Ernson rounded them up. "Nothing could have gotten past us. We're going to make another sweep. Stone, take right point as we retreat back around."

They recircled about a quarter mile. Stone saw something that wasn't right—three bamboo shoots cut when they shouldn't be cut. He walked six more paces forward and there was another bamboo shoot cut. To his left, several feet back, another was cut.
Charlie's brilliant. He never cuts more than two or three pieces at a time in one area. But he's not too brilliant because he never likes to walk more than six to eight feet away.

Nearby was a large Banyan tree, so soft it could be pulled apart. Stone motioned for the lieutenant. If they acted unnaturally, whoever was hidden there would cut them in half.

A game of pretend went by, kind of like hunting rabbits in Missouri. The little critters would sit still as a rock, and Stone would walk on by like he hadn't seen a thing, then make a big circle, come around from behind, and blow their heads off.

He circled around and motioned for French Fry to close in. He pointed to where someone had to be hiding in a ground-pit. French Fry took a grenade from his vest, pulled a pin, made it clip. Mentally,

Stone counted with him, one-one thousand, two-one thousand.

French Fry threw it in the hole. An explosion roared, spewing grass and dirt. Running to the lip, French Fry peered over the side. He turned away and threw up.

Gonzales hollered, "Get the mother out of the hole."

"I find 'em, you get 'em," Stone said. "I ain't doing it."

Ernson stepped in. "Drag it out, Stone."

Stone stepped around French Fry and his mess, and dropped on his knees. Grenades and bullets tore flesh and bone to shreds. He grabbed onto the largest piece of meat and dragged the body out. Another body was beneath the first. Stone laid them side-by-side. The sex of the first was indistinguishable, but the second looked like a young man, dressed in black pajamas and Ho Chi Minh retreads. The two of them had shared one AK47.

Gonzales knelt and went through their pockets, but found nothing.

"Sorry to disappoint you." Stone nudged the sergeant aside as he grabbed the second body. He'd drag it to the road the same way he'd dragged bucks out of the woods since he was eight.

The worst body, Stone left for Gonzales.

"It didn't mean nothing, this killing," Stone reminded himself. When he thought of that five-ton, those screams, killing these two in the hole, it didn't mean a thing.

When they reached the trucks, some were pulling the twisted five-ton to the side of the road.

"How'd the guys in the truck make out?" Ernson asked.

The GI shook his head, pointed his thumb toward the ground.

Stone kicked at the side of the road. He should have seen something before this happened. Death came with a puff of white smoke, quick as taking a breath.

They entered the vehicles slowly, somberly, some of them smelling like death. Each passed the truck pulled on the side, grateful it wasn't them.

### 

The convoy continued for several more hours. Stone never spoke to the driver. His attention stayed on their surroundings. He could taste the diesel fuel and his head throbbed, not at all helped by the driver's blaring radio. But the music broke the driver's fear, so Stone let him have it.

They reached Tan In and unloaded the vehicles. In the morning they made the trip back to Long Ben.

### 

The Wolfhounds stayed in the forty-sixth NCO area. As Stone prepared for another thirty-minute shower, he noticed how French Fry lay on his bunk, arm slung over his eyes, quiet as death.

He was from Maine and claimed to have the little man's syndrome. Every time he got drunk, he tried to whip the biggest man's ass, and always got his own ass plowed. As soon as chow was over, Stone planned on talking to the little man, maybe see what was messing with his head.

But at mealtime, French Fry didn't show. Everyone else was going to the club, but Stone went back to the barracks.

French Fry sat on a footlocker, feet flat on the floor, twisted to the side with his head buried in the crook of his arm. Just like a small bantam rooster in a cockfight.

Stone's steps were quiet as he drew near. French Fry's sobs reached his ears.

He dug the can opener out of his pocket and sat beside the kid. "Hey buddy, let's have a cool one. This place makes a man sweat in strange places."

French Fry sat straight and wiped his eyes, took a quick deep breath. Stone offered him a Falstaff. "Damn hot day."

"Sure was, man. You okay?"

French Fry shrugged his shoulders. "Yeah."

Stone started to get up.

". . . they look different dead."

Stone relaxed, took a deep drink. He propped his elbows on his spread knees, and swallowed hard. "Guess so."

French Fry's thin nostrils were bright red, the same color as the whites of his eyes. "You know, when we did this in the world, when we practiced, I threw it in the hole, and it went off and I felt good. When the thing yesterday was over, you dragged those bodies out—they were kids, man . . . and it wasn't good."

Stone threw an arm across French Fry's shoulders. He'd dated girls with more girth, girls from dairy farms who'd hauled milk cans all their lives. "A gook's a gook, don't let it sweat you. They were gonna cut you up, man. Look what they did to those guys in the truck. That could just as easy been you and me. When you tossed that grenade, you saved our lives, son. They ought to put you in for a medal."

A slow grin stretched French Fry's mouth. "You know, you're looking old, man."

Stone removed his arm from French Fry's shoulder and knocked him on the arm with the back of his hand. He was only nineteen, and calling this kid "son."

"Let's go to the club, son. You're not a virgin anymore."

### 

Mail call was the single most important event in the GI's life. Getting a letter meant they were not forgotten by people in the world. The sergeant dragged the heavy bags of mail into the open. Stone tried not to anticipate. Usually it wasn't hard, but today, he wanted to hear from home.

Was he lonely? No, this was worse. It was about hope, the salivating kind a dog does under the dinner table. If he let himself get started, where would it end? He was here, in Nam, and he couldn't afford to want more.

Too bad Jeannie had dumped him right before he'd gotten drafted. It'd be great to get a letter, smelling like perfume, written on pink stationery in her curly handwriting.

But letters from females weren't all good. He'd seen guys lose it after getting a Dear John. No, he was better off not anticipating. If Mom wrote, that was great; if not, that was better. It meant they were fine. That's all he needed to know.

Of course, he'd come to the point where he wasn't writing letters either. Putting pen to paper went something like this: "Dear Mom, my how I've changed. I kill people now. Aren't you proud of me? Dear Mom, I drag women out of holes and shoot them. Aren't you proud of me? Dear Mom, we only put three men in a chopper today. Aren't you relieved it wasn't me?"

He couldn't find any words to send home, so he wrote nothing. And he got nothing back. That war took the farm boy piece of him and crushed it.

First sergeant finished with mail call and Stone began to return to his area. "Hold on, Stone. You've got a letter from the Red Cross."

Was this how they notified you if something was wrong at

home? Stone quickly crossed to the first sergeant. "What's the deal, Top?"

Top looked pissed off. "Stone, when was the last time you wrote home?"

He pretended to contemplate the whole issue of writing home for the first time. "First week I got here."

"Your mother has written a letter to the Red Cross, asking if you're alive. Would you please write to your mother and hand it to me with the address? I will assure the company commander that you have written home. Do you understand?"

"Yes, Sergeant." Stone took the paper and pencil and scribbled, "Mom, I'm alive. Leave me alone."

He folded the paper, addressed it, and handed it to the first sergeant.

"I trust we won't have to do this again, Stone?"

"I don't think so, Top."

###

Ernson appointed Stone and Macabee to a detail in the village. As always, Stone looked forward to getting away for a few hours. They had just entered the village when he spotted a puppy. It was black and white with a pug-shaped muzzle and little wagging tail. The animal was tied beside a small hootch where a mama-san sold goods along the road.

"I want to talk to the mama-san about that dog."

Macabee laughed. "That's the old woman's dinner, man."

"We'll see."

"They eat dogs, man. Dogs and cats. You know that."

He did know, but didn't care. Stone reached in his pocket and took out a military payment certificate. He went over to the old woman and grabbed her hand, pressing ten dollars through her curled fingers.

"I want the dog." He pointed.

Beetle nuts were chewed for toothache, but they eventually rotted teeth. This mama acknowledged Stone's request with a toothless, beetle-nut grin.

Stone didn't care if Macabee laughed. He'd paid twice that to save the pup. He knew he had no heart left, couldn't even write a letter to his mother. But he couldn't allow a woman to kill a dog for a pot of dog soup.

He grabbed the puppy. It whined and licked his face until he laughed like a kid on the farm.

He and Macabee finished their business and headed back to the front gate. The guard asked them to stop so he could pet the pup. He hadn't seen one in a while.

Inside the compound, the pup caused a stir. Everyone stopped to rub its ears or let it chew on their fingers. It was the nicest day for Stone in a long time. He headed to the medic's hootch to show Doc.

"What are you going to name him?" Doc asked, feeding the

pup bits of canned eggs.

"Macabee says I ought to call him Stew, since he was headed for the cook-pot."

Doc threw back his head and laughed. "Yeah, that suits him."

Stew kind of stuck. He became the mascot for the squad.

###

Stone tried to find French Fry that evening. When he did, the little man was drunk again, passed out in the mess tent. He wanted to show him Stew, but French Fry wasn't coherent enough to be interested.

Ernson came by to get a cup of coffee. He stirred three packs of sugar into the mug. He liked the pup, was feeding him peanut butter from his fingers. "Hold on fella, those little needle teeth hurt."

Stew thought Ernson's fingers were part of the meal. "Did you put in for your promotion? You're eligible for buck sergeant. You have enough points. Time and grade can be weighed in a combat zone. I think you ought to put in for it. You're good with the men, Stone, and someday I'm going to need you."

Stone held Stew nose to nose. The pup licked his face. "We got Gonzales, Sir. He's better at this than me."

Ernson wiped the peanut butter on a napkin. "Sometimes our abilities show us the next step. You seem to fit the job."

"Thanks for the compliment, Sir. I don't want to lead anybody, anyplace. I just want to go home in one piece."

Ernson took a sip of the coffee, ran one lip over the other. "I can understand that. That's every thinking man's goal."

Chap stood, anxious to escape this conversation. "Sir, you've gotta worry about all of them. Right now, all I worry about is me."

# LONG BEN, VIETNAM, 1969
# CHAP STONE
# CHAPTER 8

"There's only one man I can really count on—good old Jim Beam."

—Ellen Porter, RN

They had a choice of three different NCO clubs at Long Ben: one for the infantry, one for the clerical, and one for the medics. With the exception of Doc, the medics' club was off limits to all of Stone's platoon. They settled for a few drinks at the infantry hootch and played a few rounds of pool.

Everyone was having a good time and drinking heavily. After drinking three cold beers, Stone decided that was enough for him. He'd not grown to like them and didn't relish getting sick again.

French Fry seemed to be doing okay, and Gonzales was revved, rapping out a beat on the table. Stone thought it was a good time to back out the door and get away. He hadn't seen Doc for a couple of days and planned to look him up.

Doc was in the medics' hootch about a half mile down the road. He let Stone into the air-conditioned building. It felt like walking into a meat cooler. All the medics wore jackets. Stone was envious. They laughed when he began to shiver.

Doc offered him a cup of coffee. Stone held the steaming cup between his hands.

They caught up on small talk. "Why don't you and I go shoot some pool at the medics' club?"

Doc changed and spruced himself up. Stone wondered why he took such pains. "Is that cologne you're slapping on your face?"

"Brut," Doc admitted, giving his cheeks a final pat.

"What are you trying to do?"

The rest of the guys started to laugh. Someone informed him, "There may be women at the club. Round-eyed women—nurses!"

Stone ran a hand over his hair. He stood behind Doc and checked his reflection in the mirror. He looked a little shabby next to Doc. His hair needed a trim and Doc's clothes were ironed, while his looked slept in.

Doc grinned at him. "Don't worry, killer. You'll do all right."

They walked down the dusty road to the medics' club. When someone pushed open the doors to leave, loud music blasted out the doorway. Inside, a group gathered around one of the pool tables. The women stood out like cut bamboo in the jungle. They wore civilian attire, and Stone found himself breathing through his open mouth.

Doc jabbed him in the ribs. "Close your mouth."

He'd been staring, and was so embarrassed he backed off to

a private corner to let things settle. It was pure pleasure to look at American women. Sure, lust was involved, but it was more, it was . . . comforting, and painful, too. He was homesick.

After several games of pool, a newcomer arrived. She wasn't attractive. Back home, he wouldn't look at her twice. She was five-foot-six or -seven with dirty blonde hair. Her face was too round, and the eyes behind her thick glasses were underscored with bags, making her look like she needed a long rest. Large, long-fingered hands handled the cue. Chap couldn't stop watching her.

She had a way of moving around the table that was confident. She carried a million stories inside. And she didn't give a damn what any of them thought about it. That was the thing. He could see it, like the tripwire against Hood's leg. She didn't give a damn because she knew the truth, just like him.

A tall, thin medic approached her, appallingly eager, making Stone wonder if he'd looked that way to Soou Ling, and to Jeannie back home.

The medic was digging scrip out of his wallet, smacking a fiver onto the green. "C'mon and give me a go. Five bucks says I can beat you."

She thunked the blunt end of her stick against the rough wood floor. "I don't know how to play."

Someone at the bar sniggered. Doc took the seat next to Stone and handed him a beer. "That girl's a nurse, and she hustles pool. She'll take that guy to school on how to play."

"No shit?"

"No shit."

The thin medic persisted.

"I don't know how to play," the nurse said again.

"I'll teach you for ten dollars. I'll tell you what, if I lose I'll give you twenty dollars. If you lose, you have to give me a kiss."

She pretended to consider the offer, but it was all bull, shining like silver, this bullshit Stone could see. "Okay. What do we play?" she asked.

"Let's play some nine ball."

"Okay, but you have to break."

The young man broke and he didn't make anything. In a blitz, the nurse made eight balls consecutively. As the nine ball set easily in the right corner pocket, she asked him, "Should I make it?"

"Where're you from?"

"I'm from Missouri. You gotta show me your stuff, boy." She sank the ball in the pocket, gingerly pushed her glasses back on the bridge of her nose and held her hand out. "Pay me."

He put the twenty MPC in the palm of her hand, and the place exploded with laughter and foot-stomping. She reached for her glass and took a big drink of what looked like Jim Beam.

"Anyone else?" she asked.

Doc kicked Stone on the knee. "Take her on."

"I don't think so."

But she'd overheard and headed Stone's way. "What's the matter, cowboy, afraid of a little nurse?"

When Stone stood, he had six inches on her. "I'll play, but you have to teach me."

"What would you like to play?"

"Eight ball. But you have to be gentle."

They played eight ball for quite a while. Finally Stone placed the cue where she couldn't hit the eight ball, high in front of the seven ball. When she tried to make the eight, she scratched, and this time the roar was for Stone. He held up his cue, and they hadn't even placed a bet.

"My name is Stone, and I'm from Missouri, too."

"Yeah? Where you from?"

"Neosho."

"Well, I'm from a smaller town than that—a little place called Bois de Art. Population fifty-eight."

Stone laughed. "I know exactly where that's at, just off of 266. My dad used to drive us through there. What's your name?"

"Ellen Porter. Friends call me Ellie."

They moved to a corner table and Stone bought her another

drink. He caught Doc's eye and winked.

"How long you been in Nam?" he asked.

"A hundred twenty-one days."

"Well, I've got just a little over two hundred seventy and counting."

"If I had that much time to do, soldier, I'd be hanging myself."

She made him laugh. He held off drinking too much, but she downed one after another, not losing her edge, or growing too loud, yet he knew she had to be plowed.

After a couple of hours Stone said, "How about we take a walk and sober up a little bit?"

They left the club and started walking. It felt strange to walk with an American woman. He could almost pretend they were on a date in the States.

"What unit are you from, Ellie?"

"The 47th EVAC here in Long Ben."

"What do you do?"

"You got a cigarette?"

He handed her one, and it took four tries to light it with the C-ration matches. Stone asked her again, "What do you do?"

"You mean you want to keep talking and not get me in the sack?" He didn't answer. She took a deep drag and blew a long stream of smoke. "When I first got here, they sent me to trauma. I was on a surgical team. We'd have three, four teams on one patient sometimes—one on the chest, some on legs, some arms, some heads." She picked a small piece of tobacco off her tongue. "I just took care of them. Before I got here . . . I was so afraid of this place . . . had nightmares. Then I learned, what you can't see . . . can't really hurt you. But what I do see . . ." she pushed the glasses up her forehead and rubbed an eye with the heel of her hand.

The tears started quietly. She threw the cigarette down and ground it underfoot. "So many die . . ." The tears came harder, but she was quiet about it.

There was the truth. Just the plain truth, and it could be ugly. The best thing would be to let it sit there and not run away from it. That would be the best thing a person could do for another, the way Doc had done with him.

"You guys save a lot of people. Have you thought of that?" he said. That was the truth too, the other side of the ugly truth.

She wiped at her cheeks. Her eyes belonged to an older woman, an ancient, sad woman. "How do you think I keep my sanity? Once you guys get here, there's only three out of a hundred don't make it. That's better odds than any trauma room in the world."

"You gotta be proud of that."

They started to walk again, a slow pace, their feet heavy.

"What do you do around here when you're not patching people up or playing pool?" She drank herself into oblivion, he'd bet. Just like tonight.

"We have this group called the Medcap—Medical Civilian Action Patrols. A couple times a month we go to the hospitals and orphanages in Saigon and try to treat as many kids as we can. We're going tomorrow, in fact."

"I'll be here tomorrow."

"Don't tell me you want to come along."

"I might. If I can get permission."

They stopped before her quarters.

"If you want to go, meet me here at my hootch tomorrow at 0800 hrs. If you can't make it . . . no big deal."

"Okay." He took her fingers, raised them to his lips, pressed a kiss against the back of her hand. He didn't know where it came from, this kiss against her rough red knuckles. He just felt like doing it.

"See you tomorrow," she said.

### 

In the hut, French Fry was passed out. Several of the other guys were too drunk to move. Gonzales sat on his bunk staring and holding a half-empty bottle. It would be futile to ask the sergeant for leave, and at 1200 hrs. it was too late to ask anyone else.

In the morning, Stone got up early and entered the first

sergeant's office, where he reported in.

"What's your problem?" the sergeant said.

"Requesting permission to spend the day with the Medcaps."

First sergeant looked taken aback. "It's your day off, just be careful."

Stone signed out and went outside the sergeant's operation area. He punched his fist in the air.

After breakfast he gathered his equipment, got a canteen full of water and a pistol belt. He still carried the 97, even though he was going to Saigon. He was in front of Ellie's quarters at 1945 hours. She came out and started loading supplies in the back of the jeep.

"Morning, soldier." She was no prettier in the harsh sunlight, but he was glad to receive her smile.

"What can I do to help?"

They began to load the jeep with bandages and supplies. They had a Meramac cooler of small vials on ice, and a bag full of small syringes.

From around the corner came Doc, another nurse, and another medic. Stone was disappointed he'd have to share Ellie's company.

Doc said, "I see Ellie has recruited you."

Stone laughed. "I don't really know what I can bring to this."

Doc shrugged. "How about candy?"

They agreed to wait while Stone ran over to the PX. The

proprietor was just opening when he got there. He bought the last four Hershey bars. These were real chocolate, not the John Wayne bars that wouldn't melt in the heat. Kids didn't like those. When the GIs handed them out, the kids were always disappointed.

He grabbed four bags of Worthies too, a pack of cigarettes, and a cold soda. Eager as a kid going on a picnic, Stone gathered his purchases and headed for the crowded jeep.

###

Just outside of Saigon was an ancient church built over a 1,000 years ago, its crumbling bell tower rising high like a broken pillar. Obviously, the church had been bombed. But the four-foot wall and chain link fence surrounding it were intact.

Doc pulled the jeep up to the cast-iron padlocked gate and honked. Children poured out the building like locusts. Several nuns followed, coming all the way to the gate, producing a huge ring of keys, opening the lock and waving them in.

Stone was used to seeing kids this age, but he'd come to be suspicious of them. Sometimes they acted as saboteurs, carrying satchel charges. But Ellie and Doc were hugging these kids, loving on them.

Ellie looked at him, brows raised. "You know, they won't bite you."

He didn't respond.

She held out her hand. "Come on, get out of the jeep."

Two French nuns stood near Ellie, chattering in broken English. Stone managed to understand they'd been at this orphanage since 1955, and the children were all victims of the war, left without parents.

Inside the church, rows of seventy beds filled it like a small hospital. In almost every bed was a child. Doc and Ellie began their tour, vaccinating, changing bandages, treating their small patients with kindness.

One of the sisters nudged Stone. "What are you doing here?"

"I'm just a friend of Ellie's. I'm in infantry."

"All these children need friends, just as you do."

Stone remembered the candy, reached in his fatigue pocket, the one that usually carried shotgun shells. His fingers closed on the four Hershey bars.

Along the wall sat a row of kids, hollow-eyed and too quiet. He approached them, holding the candy instead of his 97.

"Please, just give them a bite," the nun called after.

"They've only been here a few days. Most of them have been starved."

Stone stopped before the first little boy. His bones looked rickety, no muscle around the joints, his knees swollen, belly ready to pop. He was like a little chicken, his bones hollow like a bird's.

"Take a taste, partner." Stone slipped the bit of chocolate into the child's mouth, and the small lips closed around it.

Stone walked a little farther down the line.

"Hello, number one GI. My name is Lyn." She looked all of ten.

"Hi there, Lyn. My name is . . . Chap."

She held her arm up. It was a small stump. Tenderly he shook it like a hand.

"You have any chocolate?"

He placed a large bite in her mouth, noticed she was also missing a leg. She smiled as she chewed.

It went that way all day, from bed to bed to bed. He sat children on his lap, bounced them on his knee, threw them in the air, and gave them Worthies to suck on. When he could no longer stand to see their hurt, Stone took refuge on the porch.

Later, he watched the nuns set out their noon meal—rice with tiny bits of meat, making five fish feed a multitude. The sisters wanted to feed Stone and the medical crew, but they all refused.

He watched Doc and Ellie wrap bandages around a little girl's charred torso. They were so gentle, the little girl brave. He wanted Ellie for a friend. He thanked God Doc already was.

"Where do the clothes and food come from?" he asked one of the nuns.

She looked at the earth, dug in the dust with her bare toe. "We're no longer sponsored by the church. We get donations from strangers and people who want to help the children."

Stone was surprised. He reached in his pocket and found all the MPC scrip he had. He bowed to the sister, filled her hands with the money. She blessed him.

All the way home, they laughed and talked about what a change of pace it was to help the kids. And how sad.

Ellie twisted around in her seat, her hair whipping in the hot wind. "You should have been a medic instead of a grunt."

Stone held the 97 between his knees. "I feel more comfortable where I'm at."

When they got back to Long Ben, they unloaded the jeep. "Would you like a cold drink?" Ellie asked Stone.

Finally, it looked like he'd have her to himself. "Why sure."

Ellie had a small room. "I put beer on ice before we left this morning. The Meramac cooler keeps it cold all day."

He looked around for a safe place to lay his weapon. She saw what he wanted and motioned toward the clean towel that lay spread on the top of a metal chest she used as a dresser.

He got rid of the gun, then crushed the boonie hat between his hands. "You've got walls. Privacy."

She studied him while working a rubber band from around her ponytail. "You gonna get shy on me?"

He set the hat near the 97. "I ain't shy."

They grew quiet and he touched a strand of her hair. She must have washed it that morning. It picked up the dim light from the lamp and shone like honey.

She took her glasses off and stepped close. "Please hold me."

His arms closed around her, and she moved against him, put her head on his shoulder and sighed. "I always have a letdown after seeing the children."

He kissed her, gentle. She led him the few steps to the bed, and he followed her down.

Ellie's body wasn't perfect like Soou Ling's. He didn't gasp over her breasts, or fumble at his buckle like a kid. Knowing her made him patient. Everything he did was right, every way he touched her. He felt his heart open wide and knew he'd do anything for her. Anything.

They lay quiet together when it was over. "Chap," she whispered, "sometimes when I look into their ditty bags . . . see pictures of wives, kids . . . sweethearts . . . or they tell me stories about their families, they remind me how real they are, how human. I can't close myself off like so many do. I can't believe they're just a diagnosis, or a wound. They're like my brother . . . they're like you."

"Shh," he told her. "They ain't me. I'm me. And I'm here with you."

### 

Stone awoke in pain, thought of his gun. Who was hitting him like this, and where the heck was he?

It was Ellie, the girl he was beginning to have a deep feeling for, like love, and she was turning on him, looking wild-eyed through tangled strings of hair, grunting as she tried to move him out of her room. "Get out of here, you bastard. Get out!" She spoke through her teeth.

"What's the matter with you? What did I do?"

He grabbed his pants, shoved one leg in. She wouldn't stop pushing long enough for him to get them all the way on.

He grabbed the 97 and stumbled over the threshold. She fired the rest of his things out behind him and slammed the door. He finished tugging on his pants and whacked his fist against the door.

"Ellie, what is it? What'd I do?"

He could hear sobbing, but she wouldn't answer. Not after five minutes . . . not after twenty.

# KOOTUM, VIETNAM 1969
# CHAP STONE
# CHAPTER 9

"Dying ain't always the worst thing, hell no it ain't."

—Hatti

After Ellie threw Stone out of her hootch, he'd returned to the Quonset hut. Late morning found him sitting on his bed, staring into near space while he scratched Stew's ears.

He let Stew chew his fingers, then rolled him on his back and rubbed the fat belly. The warm fur and wet laps from Stew's tongue went straight to Stone's heart.

A dispatcher called out his name. "Stone, First Sergeant wants you front and center."

That was the last thing he wanted to hear. This was his day off. Then again, Top may have heard about the ruckus at Ellie's and wanted an explanation.

Stone got himself presentable. He hadn't been in the country long enough not to care about his appearance. As ordered, he reported to the First Sergeant. The platoon leader, Ernson, sat next to Top grinning.

"Mr. Stone, you've only been in the country a few months, but even so you've done quite well. The Lieutenant here thinks a lot of you. He sees leadership potential. What I see is a brash young man. What do you see, soldier?"

"Sir, I'm a soldier in the United States Army and I'm here to follow orders, Sir."

"I know you've been through some hard times, Stone, but you've come through okay. The Lieutenant sees something in you I tend to agree with. Because we're in a combat zone, he's placed a request for an OSP to sergeant. I'm here to hand you your Sergeant stripes."

It wasn't often that a PFC went to buck sergeant. Even still, Stone thought he'd made it clear to Ernson that he didn't want a promotion. "Sir, I . . ."

"Attenhut," Top ordered. "I want to be the first one to salute the new sergeant."

Stone briskly returned the salute, did an about face with orders in one hand, stripes in another. He walked out of the First Sergeant's office feeling a mixture of pride and despair.

The pride won over. All the way back to the hut he kept checking the stripes in his hand. When he got back to the hootch, he screamed loud enough to wake those with hangovers.

"Shut up," they yelled, throwing anything they could reach.

He had to tell Doc. Doc was in the medics' quarters, preparing to go on Medcaps again. "I just got promoted." He held the stripes for

Doc's inspection.

Doc clapped him on the back. "That's great. Congratulations. You deserve it."

They shook hands. "Hey Stone, I need to talk to you about Ellie tonight."

Stone pulled his hand away, shoved it in his pocket. "I . . . don't feel like talking about it."

Doc nodded. "I know. I'll see you when I get back."

In the Vietnamese humidity, rust could form overnight. Stone spent most of the day cleaning weapons, not about to lose the old 97 to anything, especially rust. After supper, he tried to write a letter home, but his heart wasn't in it. He couldn't get past "Dear Mom." He thought about Ellie, the vehemence with which she'd driven him away. It really hurt.

### 

That night, Stone, Neal, Hatti, R.W., Sutherland, Macabee, Hagland, and Gonzales sat around a table at the club. News of Ellie's tirade against Stone had spread. They tried to cheer him up, which was only making him feel worse.

Doc brought over a bottle of Jim Beam and sat it in the center of the table. "Take a drink, Stone, doctor's orders."

Stone shivered as it went down his throat.

"Now you stay put and listen." Doc straddled a chair.

He held a fat stogie between his fingers. "Every time Ellie starts to care about some guy, he ends up dead. She was going to get married twice in the last eight months, both times to chopper pilots. Those guys came up MIA. She worked in surgery, and she cracked, couldn't handle guys coming in with no legs or arms. When she got back from R & R, they put her in recovery. She's had a hard time, Stone. She's afraid to try again. Let's face it, the chances of any of us going home in one piece aren't great."

They sat in silence for a long time.

"Hey Doc," Neal said in his thick Louisiana accent, "do you think a man losin' a leg is worser than dying?"

Doc flicked ash from the stogie, studied the orange tip. "Sometimes it's worse."

Stone slapped the table. "You guys are doing a great job of cheering me up. Damn, I feel good."

Hatti held up his hand, "Now wait a minute. I want a pact. If something happens to one of us out there, man, we got to know our buddies won't let us go home half a man. If I lose something, and I ain't gonna be human no more, you gotta promise to take me out. I ain't gonna live in somebody's pity world. We don't go home half. We go home in one piece, or we don't go home."

They all knew the possibilities and had seen them firsthand.

Hatti leaned into the table. "If you're in on this, grab hold of the bottle." Hatti grabbed hold, followed by Neal, Sutherland, Macabee, Hagland, Gonzales, R.W. Stone put his hand over the bottle's top.

###

Several weeks went by. They enjoyed convoy duty as long as possible. Toward the end of monsoon season, the lieutenant informed them that their orders had changed. They'd be working with a group of CBEs—combat engineers—making sure they stayed alive while clearing QL 4, the sixty-second land clearing.

Everyone thought it would be a pug job. They were part of the long convoy headed toward Tay Ninh. Stone counted forty-one tractor trailers. Every third truck was guarded by a tank or track vehicle carrying eight to ten grunts.

It was something to watch the engineers operate. Their huge dozers had cages around them. Their blades pointed at forty-five degree angles and were razor sharp on the bottom for shaving Mother Earth.

Eight to ten abreast, the huge machines cleared seventy yards off the road to create a kill zone and improve the trails. At night, they circled up together like old wagon trains, with tanks on the outside.

It was Stone's job to lay out trip flares, claymores, and land mines. He thought of Charlie as a slick rabbit or a ground hog, and looked for three or four ways to catch him instead of just one. He'd put a land mine close to a trip flare. The flare would go off first, and a few minutes later they'd hear an explosion. "Got you, sucker," he'd mutter under his breath.

The engineers appreciated Stone's artwork. In the morning, Stone would go out and disarm his flares and traps. He'd give the men the A-okay. Then they'd be able to relieve themselves and get their vehicles together.

Sixty kilometers from Tay Ninh they found an old French fort called Kootum. The remnants of one crumbling wall still stood. Nearby was the mountain called Nuipa Din. It looked like it rose up in the middle of nowhere. Its top was totally flat.

Charlie owned this mountain. Rumor had it the NVA hospital was located in its depths. The U.S. could never infiltrate the series of tunnels or bypass the many traps, so they let each other pass. That was one of the strange ironies in Nam.

After eight weeks of working with the engineers, Stone and Gonzales and the platoon were heading back to Black Horse.

### 

Wherever Stone went, Stew was beside him, even when he went to the shit house. At chow, Stew got half of Stone's food.

"You think more of that dog than anyone else," Macabee teased.

Stone wouldn't deny it.

One morning Ernson called a meeting for platoon and squad leaders. "We're going to lose our home here at Black Horse. This platoon and two others are being transferred to Kootum. Our orders don't specify why."

Gonzales and Stone walked with Top and Ernson after the meeting. "There's nothin' around Kootum except Charlie," Gonzales said. "That place sits right on the Cambodian border."

Even though Ernson and Top wouldn't comment, they all knew Kootum was a prime launching site for probes and attacks.

Ernson asked, "How much do you guys know about ambush?"

"Only what we learned at AIT (Advanced Individual Training)," Stone answered. "I completed the 25th Ambush School at Scoffield Barracks," Gonzales said. "Why do you ask?"

Again, they were left in the dark.

Stone hoped R.W. was off doing detail. He wanted the hootch to himself. Just him and Stew. He didn't like this new turn of events. Black Horse wasn't much, but he'd learned to count on it being there. All he wanted to do was make it through his tour and get back to his world. He felt like the mud got muckier, pulling him in deeper.

Ambush was the most brutal form of killing. That was what this war had dissolved to—ambushes. Every night across Vietnam, hundreds and hundreds of men set up ambushes to kill Charlie, and Charlie did the same to kill GIs. The entire war, it seemed, was made up of skirmishes between groups of fifteen or twenty men, most of the time never seeing each other, only hearing and making each other fearful.

Stone remembered his dad talking about Korea. North Koreans would charge hundreds at a time, and the machine guns would mow them down.

He'd give anything to be able to see Charlie as clearly as they saw us. But Charlie wasn't going to make it that easy.

After supper, Stone approached Gonzales. The sergeant sat alone in the back corner of the mess tent, toying with his knife. Stone almost turned around twice before he reached him.

"What's on your mind?" Gonzales held the blade, as if he contemplated throwing it.

"Gonzales, teach me what you know about ambushes."

### 

The following day the company began rapid activities to move toward Kootum. It took them twenty-four hours to pack up their gear and assemble a convoy. Two days of travel would be required to get there.

It didn't take Stone long to move his possessions. He had next to nothing. All that really mattered was the 97, and Stew.

They had a squad leaders' meeting, and Ernson briefed them. "Once we arrive at Kootum, we'll secure the whole To Li Basin Complex. To do this, we'll send out patrols at ten kilometers, three-hundred-sixty degrees around the base to a point just north of Song Tree. Our mission is twofold. In the daylight we'll be looking for possible mortar and rocket sites that might pose a threat to the chopper base. We will also start establishing areas for ambushes of suspect enemy activities. To accomplish this, our platoon will be group A, Nuipa Din south. Stone, you'll head group A."

Once they reached Kootum, they searched the area for a week, until they could find no more mortar or rocket sites for activity. Charlie was there, but they hadn't been able to find him yet.

The surveillance continued for several weeks. On the ninth day, Gonzales and Stone determined they'd found a significant trail. Ernson called in the specific grid coordinates so aerial photographs could be taken.

"Why do you think this trail is well used?" Ernson asked the two men.

"Look, Lieutenant, they're wearing Ho Chi Minh retreads. That's what makes the brief, short, tire prints. Charlie wears the tires we throw away. He's got a shoe with a fifty-thousand-mile warranty," Gonzales said.

"There's lots of traffic through here," Stone continued. "They're making a new rice paddy about ten meters from the edge of the jungle. An irrigation trench was dug right next to the trail, but it has lots of vegetation in it. They have to take the trail to get around this new paddy. When they do . . ."

"We fucking-A let them have it," Gonzales said with a hint of hatred in his voice.

Forty-eight hours later Ernson informed them they were going on an ambush trail. "This is what we're going to need. Gonzales, get five claymores. Sutherland, get smoke grenades in red, blue, and green. Stone, get a case of AC grenades. We want two bandoleers of 79 rounds. I want two to twenty bandoleers per man. I want all eight of you to carry the 16. That includes you too, Stone. You leave the shotgun here or carry them both, I don't care. We're going to be gone at least five days. You'll know where we're going when we get there."

They had two hours to get their stuff together. Stone was not comfortable taking only five claymores. He took two extra, plenty of copper wire, and heavy black thread for setting booby traps.

They flew out of Kootum in two Hueys with support vehicles on the ground. The forty-five-minute ride was a real treat. Stone recognized the terrain. They were headed right back to the high-traffic trail.

"We're going to spread ourselves thin," Ernson told them after they'd landed, "and we're going to sit and watch this trail. We're going to watch it like our lives depend on it, because they do. We're not going to shoot anybody, we're going to watch for the next five days. We'll work in groups of three. Stone, take yours a hundred meters to the right. Gonzales, you head to the other side of the paddy on the left. I'll be in the middle. Sutherland, you keep the Prick 25 here with me."

They reached their appointed places and hunkered down for the supreme monotony of watching through heat, flies, and mosquitoes.

About 0130 hrs., Stone punched Hatti. He held up all ten fingers, meaning ten men wearing black uniforms were coming down the trail.

He couldn't tell if they were men or women in their "Tom Terrific" rice hats. They all smoked to keep the mosquitoes away, and were bent forward carrying something heavy on their backs. It looked like small drums, maybe fuel for vehicles or weapons. Stone logged everything he saw.

Night two, almost exactly the same thing. Stone wondered why Ernson didn't have them set their traps now? Why did they have to wait? Obviously there were rules, even in ambushes.

On the third night, Ernson decided it was time to set the mines. It was a clear, comfortable night with a temperature in the mid-seventies, a gentle breeze, and nearly a full moon. The lieutenant grabbed a stick to draw out the plans for the squad. "To the west is the line of bamboo that no one can penetrate. That's why we have a trail in the elephant grass about ten meters out from the jungle. As they come out, we want to create a crossfire from three points. Stone, you go south to the point the trail begins to bend west. Your fire will come across toward the northeast. Gonzales, you'll set up four claymores on the trail. The first two will be for initial impact and maximum kill. The third and fourth will be set up to take out any stragglers. In addition, you will have the M79 with some willie perter and H/E. Use the H/E for anything heading back into the retreat line. Your fire will run directly west. You will have four M16s with you for cleaning up stragglers. I'll be at the corner and direct my fire almost directly north to northeast. This ambush should give us a kill zone of twenty-five to forty meters. Our escape will be directly to the east just as we came in. I have the smoke for pick up. I'll need to call in one more time to get the go for this."

At 1700 hrs. the Lieutenant called HQ for additional orders. He was given the go-ahead.

Gonzales and Stone set the claymores. Stone tied one to a tree, slightly above waist level, covering it with bits of vegetation. The second was placed in front of the tree on its tripod stand and hidden in the grass. Gonzales placed his mines in a similar fashion.

With Ernson's three-point crossfire, the ambush reminded Stone of coyotes killing cattle. But, he didn't like having only one exit if things went bad. All of his life he'd observed nature. Instinct told him one escape route wasn't enough. At the very least it should be mined to give them adequate time to make their exit.

Stone got the lieutenant's permission to advance.

"Sir, requesting permission to mine our escape route."

Ernson sighed. "Oh hell, Stone, permission granted, as long as you inform the entire squad where the mines are located."

Stone ran to the exit trail. Quickly, he dug out the smallest amount of earth and set the first mine under a fallen log. He placed the clacker cord onto the detonator and ran it seventy-five feet down the trail to a large tree. The second claymore he placed seven feet high in the fork of a tree. Again using the dark cord, he secured it, and ran the cord as far away as possible, hiding the clacker in the growth.

Charlie would have to look a long time to find the mines or clackers in the dark. He broke a limb and bent it to point toward the clacker, as an extra warning sign to himself and the platoon.

At 1745, everything was set. Stone was not yet satisfied, but he didn't have much choice. The lieutenant motioned for everyone to get ready.

Stone watched Doc get into position. He knew Doc hated this even more than the rest of them, but understood his duty. If they needed Doc, he'd be there.

At 2145, they heard someone coming down the trail. Instead of the usual party of ten, this was a small party of four, laughing and talking without a care in the world.

Ernson was pissed. He'd set this up to get maximum kill. Stone hoped he'd let them pass, they didn't look more than fifteen or sixteen years old. But he could sense Ernson's indecision—to kill them, or let them pass, to kill them, or let them pass.

Ernson raised his fist, flushed it tight, pulled it down. With that, Gonzales hit the clacker. The first two men flew in the air. From the knees up, their bodies disintegrated. Two seconds later the second mine blew. The other men were dead before they hit the ground.

The deafening aftermath roared across the jungle. The platoon hadn't fired a shot. Ernson called HQ and informed them of the contact, that they'd made several kills. He was instructed to police the bodies for any useful information.

Gonzales, Macabee, and Hagland were sent in to do the cleanup. Stone was ordered to maintain cover.

Gonzales had an eager set to his shoulders. No sooner had he bent to search the remains when the unmistakable three-round plague sounded. Macabee and Hagland dove into the trench.

Gonzales was down. He didn't scream, but they knew he'd been hit.

Stone had seen this before when deer hunting. The bucks would send three or four does out to see if there was danger while the big sons-of-bitches stayed in the back. Charlie had sacrificed four soldiers, and now Stone and the platoon were in for a hell of a firefight.

Green tracers zipped across Stone's right and left. He dropped the 16 and threw the shotgun to his shoulder. Wherever a tracer originated, he countered with several blasts from the shotgun. He directed R.W. to heave in some 79 rounds.

Ten or twelve VC were closing in on Macabee and Hagland. Stone waited for them to get even with the claymore. He punched the clacker so hard it split the skin on his palms.

There was only the roar, a giant death keel, shaking a man's core. Then silence bled into their ears hot and painful.

"Stone," Ernson called, "get Gonzales."

By degrees Stone reached Gonzales. It looked like a bear had ripped away a chunk right above his elbow. The bone gleamed white while arterial blood spurted, making a slick stain on the ground. Gonzales was in shock, unable to talk.

Eight VC were dead. Stone whispered for Macabee and Hagland to come out of the trench. In seconds, the rest of the squad set up a perimeter around the site.

Stone felt a hand on his shoulder. Doc knelt beside him. He tied off the artery, gave Gonzales a shot for pain, and packed the wound, working his magic, talking in a voice as healing as any medicine, making them all think everything would be okay.

While Stone waited for Ernson to give orders, he wondered if Ellie would be on duty when they brought Gonzales in. This was what she was afraid of, men in bloody bits and pieces. He met her ghost and couldn't blame her for the way she was, for wanting to protect herself from a grunt like him.

What if he was hurt too, and didn't even know it? Frantically, Stone ran his free hand over his side, across his chest, down his legs. "Get ahold of yourself, man. You're all right. You're all right," Stone told himself in his most assuring voice.

The Lieutenant was ordered to pull back to the designated extraction zone. "We need to be there by daylight. It's going to be a long haul with our casualty. Let's get moving."

Macabee and Hagland managed to get Gonzales on his feet. He was going to have to walk three quarters of a mile to the landing zone. They left the eight VC to the flies. Macabee took point and Stone took drag. He disarmed one of his extra mines and packed it in his rucksack. The other he kept on line, just in case. This war was a waiting game, like hunting ground hogs. The ones who poked their noses out first got sent to the happy hunting grounds.

It took two hours to get to the LZ. Stone heard the chopper thirty seconds before the Prick 25 crackled. They were asked to pop a green smoke grenade.

He was the last one to board the chopper. Once he glanced at Gonzales and saw the fear in his eyes and the tears. He looked out the door, over the open country. He'd never liked Gonzales. He'd hated him actually. "It didn't mean nothing. None of it did," Stone said to himself. "But God, I'm just gonna ask you this, then I ain't going to ask you no more. Be kind to the bastard today. Help him out. Amen."

###

They returned to Kootum tired and hungry and one man short. The following morning, Ernson came to the platoon meeting.

"Stone, you're the new platoon sergeant, until we get somebody else with more rank. You've got twenty-four hours to clean up, pack up, and get ready to go on another ambush detail."

"We've just been gone four days, Lieutenant, and two weeks before that. Don't you think we deserve a couple days off?" Sutherland asked.

"Yeah, I do, but it ain't gonna happen. Sergeant Stone, take care of your men."

Stone shook his head. "You heard him, guys. First thing is, get your weapons clean. If they're wet, you're dead."

They began to clean their weapons, then clean their bodies and fill them with food. For the first time in several months, they'd lost somebody close. The law of averages might be catching up with them.

### 

Stone became good at ambush, because he could wait, he could feel what was going on, he could see better than most. Ernson asked Stone to take his crew on a long-range patrol for an ambush just south of Tay Ninh mountain. "You'll have eight men."

"We flying in or walking, Sir?"

"How's your shoes, Stone?"

That answered the question. Stone called a platoon meeting

and got the standard issue—five to seven claymores, H/Es, three smoke grenades, twenty clips, a couple of flashlights, and some rations.

They began their long walk before six in the morning, right at daylight. Walking across the rice paddies kicked up mosquitoes and stirred leeches that kept their calves bloody.

At 1715 hours, they had readied themselves at the designated ambush area. They hadn't been there forty-five minutes when Hagland reported movement along the woods. Stone looked through the scope. Pajamas walked along the edge of a trench in the moonlight.

Charlie laughed and joked with no regard for danger. Four men walked directly toward Macabee. Fearing Charlie might detect the ambush, Macabee detonated one of the claymores. In a roar of oil and smoke, Charlie's pointman disappeared. Sutherland radioed the company that the ambush had sprung early. The rest of the platoon began firefight on the right flank. Several of Charlie's forces could be seen running toward a treeline. The men launched 79 canister rounds to no avail.

Stone listened through the quiet and motioned for Hatti, R.W., and Macabee. They were to police the area, check out the kill zone. They found five pajama-clad bodies. Hatti was rolling one over when Stone heard the explosion.

"No." That was all Stone could say, as if one word could change anything. He ran to where the explosion had occurred. Hatti was on the ground, bloody, fragmented.

Macabee put a hand against Stone's chest, as if to hold him away. "Charlie put a grenade under his dead. When Hatti rolled him over . . . it went off."

Stone's 97 clattered to the ground.

God, Hatti, you knew better. You knew better. You ain't supposed to die on me, man. You ain't supposed . . .

Hatti moaned. Stone dropped to his knees, got his arms around Hatti's shoulders. A single tear had carved its way from the outer corner of Hatti's eye to the side of his nose. It made a clean track in the black camouflage smudging his cheeks.

"God," Stone pressed his cheek against Hatti's forehead. "Why'd you do that, Hatti?"

A leg was gone. Hatti in bits . . . "not human no more." Stone wanted to scream, and shake him.

Hatti looked at him, his gray eyes flat. Stone gripped him more firmly, but he slipped away, moved out of his body. Out of Vietnam.

### 

Stone straddled a fence between gratitude that he was alive and guilt over the air he breathed. He wrote Hatti's family and sent one of the dogtags he'd ripped from Hatti's neck with the letter.

It didn't matter if he lived or died. He quit caring one way or the other. That was a strange place to live, but it made him fearless. They said there were three stages for a grunt—apprenticeship, brashness, then fear for his short time. Stone knew they'd call him brash, but he didn't care.

The brashness made him feared.

The Company Commander thought Stone and his platoon were the best thing to happen to Vietnam since Bob Hope. Stone's squad was the only one that consistently provided him with real body counts for the daily reports.

They'd been on ambush duty for four and one half months, longer than anyone they knew of. Ernson had been right about Stone; he had special abilities. He was simply the best hunter in the company.

Stone felt proud that his platoon could kill so easily. He learned from Charlie. The greatest danger in war wasn't what you saw so much as what might get you around the next bend, or behind the next tree. In an ambush, the enemy could be killed quickly with minimal risk, or hurt badly enough that someone else could kill them. Charlie had almost stopped the largest army in the world, one ambush at a time.

This was Charlie's game, a game of fear. He'd been perfecting it for centuries. Fear caused mistakes, and mistakes slowed you down, and slowing down meant you were vulnerable for attack.

But for the ones who could hold their fear at bay, or detach from it as Stone had learned to do, the ones who became brash, they were the players, earning their stripes in ruthlessness and the art of survival.

After Hatti's death, Stone began leaving calling cards at the scene of his kills. He tore bits of paper until all that was left was the shape of a doll. Eventually, he used only black paper and added rice hats to his creations.

The dolls were dropped onto the bodies he left behind, bodies that were sometimes mutilated, keeping Charlie out of Stone's version of heaven, sometimes they were shot in the chest; that was the thing, stop them in the chest because Charlie's dangerous if he's breathing, so, stop his breathing.

Did Mom ever dream, when she'd showed Chap how to make the dolls one Christmas when money was scarce, that he'd use them halfway around the world to mark his kills?

Well, life was damn funny sometimes.

###

Rumor had it that the army fed them right two times a year—Thanksgiving and Christmas. Since today was Thanksgiving, Stone and Doc anticipated the traditional hot meal. They sat on the berm, drinking a beer.

"Hard to believe we've been here eight months." Doc took off his glasses and rubbed the dark red indentations on the bridge of his nose.

"Seems like eight years," Stone said, no humor in his voice.

Doc gave him one of his quiet looks, making him feel like an alien.

"How many ambush details you been on in the last four months?"

Stone patted Stew's head, held his muzzle closed, and growled, "Around thirty-five."

"Maybe you should tell Ernson you need a break."

They didn't speak for a while. A new recruit walked up the side of the berm and started to address Stone.

"Don't even," Stone said, not looking at the kid. "Get your ass out of here. If I want you, I'll let you know, 'Cruit."

"Yes Sir," the kid all of eighteen answered, his fair complexion already a bright red from the sun.

Doc dug a pack of crushed crackers from his breast pocket and fed them to Stew. "You know they call you Pop?"

Stone knew. He wasn't any older than most of the 'cruits that came in, but they called him Pop when they thought he couldn't hear.

They didn't know he heard everything—Charlie breathing under brush piles in the jungle, his mother crying because he couldn't write, Ellie sobbing on the other side of her door, all the screams trapped inside of Gonzales, Hatti breathing his last shaky breath. And it didn't mean shit.

"They probably call me worse than that," he said.

Stone heard it first, the unmistakable high-pitched shrill of incoming mortar. He grabbed Stew and they ran between the berm and the fifty-five gallon barrels filled with dirt and sand.

With each impact Stone clenched Stew to his chest. The first round hit outside the perimeter, throwing dirt and dust high in the air. The second hit ten meters closer toward the compound. The third hit the berm about twenty-five meters to Stone's left. The forth hit inside the berm only a few feet inside the compound, and the fifth was a good way in.

When the dust settled, Stone heard R.W. calling his name. Still carrying Stew, he and Doc met R.W. near the mess tent. "That fifth one landed right where we live," said R.W. He was right the bunker was just a smoking hole.

"Damn." Stone couldn't believe his luck. He could just as easily have been lying on his cot. Why did his luck hold when so many others' hadn't?

"Let's get us one of those cold beers they flew in for the holiday." Doc had his hand on Stone's arm, tugging him toward the mess tent.

"Yeah. Why not," he said.

### 

Two days later, they sat at chow, finishing off one of Rabid's uninspired meals. R.W. had a way of hunkering over his plate that really annoyed Stone. Couple that with the way he kept scraping his fork against the metal dish, and Stone was ready to punch him in the face.

"Knock it off before I shove that fork up your ass, R.W."

R.W. laid the fork down, put the flats of his hands on the table, and stood. He briskly saluted Stone on his way outside.

Stone looked around the tent. The short-timers were laughing to themselves, but the 'Cruits couldn't hold his gaze. He wiped his mouth and went out.

Doc caught up with him before he reached his new quarters. "Why don't you go in the village? A good whore can quiet a man's nerves."

###

Sergeant Reitner held the bottle of Jim Beam Stone had just given him. "Anything happens to that truck, Stone, and I'll take it personal."

"Nothing's going to happen to your truck. It'll be a quick run there and back. Safe and sound."

Reitner nodded, already opening the whiskey.

Stone put the other four bottles of Beam on the front seat of the five-hundred-gallon water truck. On his way out of the compound, he stopped at the gate. The MP walked over to the cab. "Where you going?"

"To get water for the showers. It's been over three weeks since I've had a wash."

The MP motioned for the gate to be lifted.

When he reached Tay Ninh, Stone stopped at the first brothel.

In the bar, he asked to see the owner. Using the last of his personal stash, he began to barter for the oldest profession on earth.

### 

Back at the compound, Stone pulled the truck to the back side of the berm. He parked it, jumped up on the tank, and flipped the lid.

"Beaucoup hot, Beaucoup hot."

"You number ten thousand GI for sticking us in here."

He laughed when he saw how upset the four girls were. They dripped with sweat and water that was left over in the tank. All of their makeup had washed off, making them look younger than he realized.

"Now settle down, girls." He patted the air with his hands. One of the girls scooped dirt and threw it at him. Another kicked him in the leg and made him limp.

Stew charged, growling and showing his teeth, a barking rescue team.

Macabee and Doc saw the ruckus and came to investigate. They caught Stone rubbing his leg. "You can have your short time with the pick of the litter for ten bucks MPC. I figured if I needed it, everyone else did too."

# QL 4, VIETNAM, MID-DECEMBER 1969
# CHAP STONE
# CHAPTER 10

"I saw an angel cover his face, then the death mask gently took its place."

—Chap Stone

Stone dragged his feet down the bunker steps. It had been days since he'd really slept. He took a right around the barrels. Hagland sat on his bunk cleaning his weapon, smiling from ear to ear. A dozen candles were being lit. Macabee played a southern hillbilly tune on his guitar.

It had been several days of guard duty for Stone. Sergeant of the guard was never easy. He sat down and took off his boots. "This is a hell of a way to make a living."

Macabee laughed and composed a wordy song. "I'm down to thirty days before I'm heading home. Underground's where you'll find me. I'm one of the few, far and in-between getting out of here with my ass intact. Underground's where you'll find me. The good Lord has taken care of me. I'm meant to be. Don't need no medals. Just want my ass to get on that freedom bird. Till then, underground is where you'll find me."

"Hate to tell you this, Mac, but I'm two days shorter than you are," Sutherland said. They cackled together.

"I'm so short," Macabee said, "Stone's gonna have to get me a ladder to crawl into my boots in the morning."

Someone chucked a can of cold beer at Stone. He cranked it open and took a long swallow.

The U.S. and the North Vietnamese decided to hold peace talks in Paris. There weren't any ambush details. They were on stand-down, nothing but guard duty and Mickey Mouse details.

War had turned boring. Stone hated fighting, but guard duty and the hot monotony had their own downsides.

Doc entered. "Top just came in on a chopper with some hot chow for tonight. There's a mail call."

This was the first call in several days. The men were excited. After the short message he'd sent his mother, Stone didn't expect anything. He wasn't worth writing to, and it was best she knew it.

With slow movements, Stone undressed. The skin on his legs was blistered from the dust and burned like fire. Doc looked at them, but there wasn't much anyone could do for jungle rot.

Grabbing his only clean towel, Stone wrapped it around his hips and found his flip flops to wear to the shower. Outside, he got a gallon of water. He'd grown proficient at getting clean, and using the Vietnamese lye soap the mosquitoes didn't like.

When he finished, everyone returned from mail call and were

kicked back on their bunks. Someone turned on a tape player with Elvis crooning he'd have "a blue Christmas without you." This had to be Macabee's music. A small package sat on Stone's bed.

"Who's this for?"

Doc said, "Looks to me like Santy Claus is coming early."

Stone wiped himself dry and pulled on his fatigue pants. He sat on the bed and held the package. It'd been mailed September 12th from his hometown and had taken nearly three months to find him. "Who'd send me something?"

The ragged brown wrappings came away easily. One corner of the box was crushed. Inside were two round containers covered with Christmas decorations. On top of one was a card with a picture of Santa Claus.

He recognized his mother's writing: "You're not forgotten, my son. Mom and Dad."

Except for Elvis, it had grown quiet. No one would look at Stone. He stared at the card and remembered how it felt to be in Mom's kitchen.

"What the hell's in those things?" Doc broke the silence.

Stone tossed the card aside and opened the small box. "Look at this, a Norelco electric shaver. There ain't a plug-in for forty miles."

They all died laughing.

Macabee lay on his back, knees in the air, cigarette between thumb and finger. "Maybe we can get a gook with a bicycle and a generator so you can shave like an executive."

"An electric shaver in a firebase in the middle of the jungle," Stone said. "Man, if my mom could only see it."

"Open that container." Doc was as excited as if the gifts were for him.

Stone pulled the plastic tape from around the lid. Inside was a homemade fruit cake. "She makes these every year." He leaned close and breathed deep. How powerful to breathe the scent of home in this place. He missed Mom. "God, I missed her," he thought.

The cake had spent so many months in the heat that it had dried out. Yet it was unthinkable to let it go to waste. "If we don't eat this now, the rats will have it before morning. Let's dig in."

They got spoons from their mess kits. Some got nuts and cherries. They laughed at how good it tasted, even dry. Fruitcake, cold beer, Christmas, and thoughts of home could not help but make one homesick for a moment.

These weren't entirely comfortable feelings, but they had merit. Eight months was a long time to be away. Macabee and Sutherland were going home. It would be grand to see them get out of Nam alive.

Like Stone, R.W. had been pulling lots of guard duty. He'd just gotten back to the bunker. "What's going on? Partying without me?"

"Don't you think it's time to get your haircut, R.W.?" Stone jibed.

"Hell no. I'm gonna go home looking like Elvis," he said, playing an air guitar and wiggled his thick hips.

They laughed and had a good time. "Get over here and get the last of this cake," Stone said.

By the time Ernson came down, there was nothing left. "I have some good news, and I have some bad news."

"Lieutenant, you're always good-newsing and bad-newsing us to death. I'm so short, I ain't leaving this bunker," Macabee stretched on his bunk, hands stacked beneath his head.

Ernson smiled, "You might change your mind when you hear what I've got to say. Which you want first, guys?"

It was unanimous. They wanted the good news.

"You guys have been in the field so long, the old man thinks you need seven days of R & R. This whole squad is going to Camron Bay."

They went nuts, square-dancing together, Sutherland walking on his hands, Macabee standing on his cot picking out a fast tune on the guitar. To the world, R & R meant rest and relaxation. But to Stone and his crew, it meant I & I, intoxication and intercourse.

"However," Ernson continued, "there is one piece of bad news. Because someone illegally stole a water truck from the engineers and brought in some illegal aliens for a romp around Thanksgiving, that person must 'fess up and keep his ass on the compound."

Here it was mid-December. The whole place was going for I & I. Stone knew that if he didn't confess, none of them would be allowed offbase.

"Lieutenant, it's been a month almost. Why does the old man want to know about the whores today?" Doc asked.

"The captain's pissed because it took him three weeks to hear about the incident. The old man feels like someone is laughing behind his back. He's got to save face, guys. So either one or two stay or . . ."

"Lieutenant," Stone interrupted, "I don't need to go anyway. Tell the old man he's got his punk. I did it, and I'm proud of it. If he don't like it . . . he's a faggot."

Ernson laughed. "Looks like you and I have guard duty for seven days while these fools are off. See the rest of you back on the nineteenth. Your chopper leaves in thirty minutes."

### 

It was chaos. The squad packed and tried to come up with cash to spend on the sins of the flesh.

"Stone, don't suppose you could lend me some money?" Doc asked. "I mean, it's too bad you can't go, but since you're not . . ."

Every month, Stone put most of his money in a savings account, keeping out a hundred bucks. "How much you need?"

"Whatever you can spare."

"I haven't spent anything in awhile. I got two hundred seventy dollars. Go ahead and take it."

Doc squeezed Stone's cheek. "I love you, baby."

When they were gone, Stone began a week of guard duty with Ernson. The cease-fire worked well, and the whole week was quiet.

On December 19th, the troop returned, sick-drunk, hungover, and looking dead. R.W. had gotten a haircut at a Vietnamese barber. He'd wanted a flat top, but was so drunk he kept tilting his head. The flat top was two inches high on the left and a quarter inch high on the right. It had been that way for four days, and Stone was the first one to notice.

Everyone had a story. They'd seen nurses, and the ocean had been warm. Stone listened and lived vicariously.

Macabee couldn't believe they'd made him and Sutherland come back. He was hoping they'd let them stay at Camron Bay since their time was so short, but cease-fire or no, they were back in the war zone.

Doc was looking thin. His shirt was misbuttoned, and a dark splotch darkened his shoulder. "Hey, Stone, I didn't forget you, partner. Got you a Christmas present." In his palm was an ivory Buddha on a gold chain. "It's for good luck, blessed by a Buddhist monk. The man told me if you wear this, bullets can't hurt you."

"In that case, give me two." Stone looped it around his neck.

"Thanks Doc, I appreciate it."

"Thanks for the money. I'll give it back to you soon as I can."

Stone welcomed the noise in the bunker. Not having the guys around had made him realize how much he cared.

As they took off their fatigue jackets, ready to go back to the grind, Stone noticed each one of them had the same tattoo. "What did you guys do that for?" he asked.

R.W. said, "They got those just for you, Stone. This is your tattoo. It's a skull and crossbones. I'm holding off getting mine until you can go, too."

"R.W., you're so full of shit," Macabee called across the bunker. "You were scared shitless of that needle. Should've seen him, Stone. No matter how much booze we poured down his throat, couldn't get the sucker anywhere near that chair."

On the top left was the word "AMBUSH"; on the right, "DEATH"; beneath, "1st of the 27th C Company."

R.W. nudged Stone. "Don't listen to Macabee. Next time we go to I & I, you and me will get one."

"R.W. knew his mama would kick his ass if he came home with a tattoo on his arm," Macabee continued. "She don't want nothing marring that soft pink flesh on her baby boy."

It was good to have them home, good to feel the relaxation of the past two weeks.

Ernson had gone to a neighboring village for charcoal. Tonight they were having steaks the guys brought back. Barbecued steak and cold beer. God certainly loved them today.

### 

Stone's troop stood in formation for roll call. Top was in exceptionally good spirits. When he finished his business, he turned the front-and-center over to Captain Collins. "I have received permission to send thirty guys from this company to Long Ben to see Bob Hope's Christmas show. Each of the four platoons can send eight. They will be escorted by convoy. Kootum will be greatly represented by the troops we send."

There were eleven in Stone's squad, counting the newbies. Ernson told Stone to pick men who'd been in the field the longest, being sure to include Macabee and Sutherland. Those two could finish their last twenty days in Long Ben before going back to the world.

When Mac and Sutherland heard the news, they threw their hats in the air and yelled. They were heading home.

Counting himself, there were seven candidates from Stone's platoon, Doc made eight, and four guys from another squad made twelve. Stone held eight small sticks the same length and four short. Everyone drew from the cluster. The last stick left was short, and that was Stone's. Doc, R.W., and a kid from the other squad came up short, too.

"You know, I was drawing for you, Stone. I'm too broke to leave the base. Looks like you're not meant to get out of Kootum," Doc told Stone. Hagland offered to give Stone his spot since he'd missed the I & I trip to Camron Bay.

"Thanks, buddy, but you go on." Stone didn't mind staying back with Doc.

The next morning, Ernson instructed the winners they'd leave at daylight on the 24th, Christmas Eve. "Look your best, take one set of clean clothes, if you have them. You'll stay at Long Ben at battalion headquarters and be gone about four days."

December 24th, everyone got up early and made their formation at 0600 hrs. Charlie hadn't sent his message in so many nights, they'd been getting real rest. After formation, French Fry, Neil, Hagland, and the others headed to the trucks. R.W., Stone, and Doc shook Macabee's and Sutherland's hands.

"If you ever see me in the world," Macabee said, "please don't tell me that you know me," and then they hugged. Stone licked Sutherland's ear for old times, and they parted laughing.

The front vehicle was an APC—amphibious vehicle on tracks. Second was a five-quarter with an M60 machine gun behind it. Third was a five-ton truck with racks in the back to bring supplies to Kootum. The fourth was a two-and-a-half-ton truck—a troop carrier. The fifth vehicle was a five-ton truck with a quad 50, originally an anti-aircraft gun.

Every man had his M16, ten clips, and for the most part wore their flack jackets and steel pots. They threw a cooler of beer in the back, and were ready to see Bob Hope.

Stone watched them exit the compound. "So long, guys."

### 

0830 hrs, the first call came over the radio. Ernson ran down in the bunker to get Stone. "They've been ambushed."

Stone reached above him, grabbed the 97 and his bandoleer of ammo and followed the Lieutenant up the stairs. R.W. had just come back from the latrine.

"We're going out," Stone yelled. "They've been ambushed."

It took about ten minutes to get ready. The captain spread a map on the hood of a truck. "Where the hell's this place at, Stone?"

Stone ran a finger over the map, looking for the point of ambush. "Exactly in front of Nuipa Din Mountain. If we follow them in by vehicle, we're likely to get ambushed ourselves. We need choppers to make a sweep on both sides, see what we've got. It's going to take us fifteen minutes to get there. They can make the sweep and radio to us."

A line of vehicles were hastily assembled—a tank, two APCs, a truck, two quad 50 five-quarters with a 60 in the back, and two or three jeeps. Fifteen minutes had passed since the first call—a damn long time to be in an ambush. The convoy had been only six miles down the road when they'd been hit. Overhead, four choppers flew three-sixties banking back and forth. One of them lost its rockets. Stone heard the explosions, saw the smoke rise in the air.

The ride seemed like an eternity. At first sight, it seemed the convoy had been reduced to flames and smoke. They passed the last vehicle of the original convoy.

The mountain was on the left. The tank went in that direction and began firing its machine guns, though there was nothing to shoot. Ernson pointed for Stone to take his squad and flank to the right.

There was no gunfire. They moved in very cautiously, afraid of an ambush within an ambush. The APC, the lead vehicle, had run over a huge mine, probably a five-hundred-pound bomb judging from the eight-foot-wide, three-foot-deep crater that threw the vehicle on its side.

The second truck had been hit by an RPG and was blown in half. The quad 50 was on its side. The only vehicle that wasn't turned over was the two-and-a-half-ton truck Stone's squad was in. They'd taken up defensive positions to return fire.

The first body was Macabee's, twisted, broken, and dead. He'd said he was meant to be, that God had blessed him.

An arm's length away was Sutherland. His face was gone.

Hagland still held his 16, his eyes wide open, like he'd seen death coming. His face was frozen in fear. Neil lay facedown. Thank God they didn't have to look at him, too.

About fifteen meters farther up was French Fry. His shock of blonde hair was the only thing identifiable. He groaned and cried like a baby. "Medic!" Stone screamed while running to help hold him. His middle was pink, red, and pulsing.

"God, it hurts. You promised you wouldn't let me hurt, Stone."

Tears streaked French Fry's muddy face. Stone realized they were his.

"Where the hell is Doc? Medic!"

"The pact . . . you promised. Oh God, help me."

"Hang on, buddy." Stone touched the 97 at his side.

"Do it," French Fry begged.

Stone laid him down, put both his hands on the gun, raised on one knee, pulled back his elbows. "Oh God, do it."

He centered the barrel near French Fry's forehead. "It don't mean nothing. Do it, you son of a bitch. Do it, you bastard. It don't mean nothing. It don't mean nothing," Stone repeated to himself.

He waited for the cold place, the place where he heard no voice but his own, calling all the shots, making all the rules, deciding who lived and who died.

But the cold place wouldn't come. He was in a bloody river,

and it was warm on his hands, and he knew, God he knew, that all this death was wrong, that French Fry's guts didn't belong in his lap, that it was wrong to put them there, obscene, horrible, and he didn't want to be a part of death any longer. He knew there was a limit inside of him, a line that wasn't obliterated no matter how thin he'd stretched it, pushed against it; they were human beings and everything mattered, every tiny minuscule pain had import, had meaning and mattered, and oh God, how could he bear it?

Life belonged to God. And death belonged to God. And French Fry did, Mac, Sutherland, Hagland, Neil . . . and himself, even the gooks. "God help me, even the gooks," cried Stone.

Chap's arms trembled, and he lowered the gun. "I can't. I'm sorry."

French Fry's throat worked convulsively. Chap dug his hands beneath his slight shoulders, pulled French Fry onto his lap, and cradled him like a baby. "I won't leave you. It'll be okay. I'll be with you."

French Fry's blood turned cold and sticky on Chap's hands by the time Doc came. Doc put two fingers on the carotid artery, and checked French Fry's pulse.

"Let him go, Stone. We got more."

There were thirty-three dead. Four barely hanging on. Stone carried French Fry to the chopper. A body with no spirit, or soul, was the heaviest thing a man could carry. Even one as small as French

Fry's.

There were no body bags. Stone laid him on the metal floor. His blood made a sucking sound as Stone turned the body onto its side, next to Mac, Sutherland, Hagland, Neil—his family.

They raised the dead into the air. They were all going home now. Stone watched until the Huey lifted off the ground and was out of sight.

Then he found his 97.

###

R.W. sat beside the road, his 16 at his feet. He looked vacant, without feelings, even hate.

Ernson got orders over the Prick 25. "We're to make a sweep of the villages between here and Kootum."

There was only one small village, and they knew it well, had been through it hundreds of times, had bought charcoal there for the steaks the guys had brought from Long Ben.

"The gooks who did this are back in the mountains where we can't touch them," Stone told Ernson.

"We've been ordered the other way, Stone. We're to make a sweep."

The rest of the company, sixty-five to ninety men walking fifteen meters apart, began the sweep. It was less than three miles back to the village.

Stone took point. If he was going to walk back to the VC, he wasn't going to get blown away triggering a booby trap.

On the surface, the whole company seemed numb. But underneath the quiet was rage. They'd just seen their best friends butchered during a cease-fire.

The condition of the trail told Stone it had recently been used. Several limbs were broken in place. But nothing indicated any mass movement.

It didn't really matter. They had orders to follow, even if they made no sense.

###

The village consisted of about twenty or so grass huts. Stone swept three men to drag all the villagers out, screaming and hollering the whole time. Huddling together, the villagers chattered with fear. The soldiers found nothing in the huts.

But something bothered Stone. There was a fire burning in the high heat of day, yet nothing was cooking. Near the fire, a piece of black cloth showed, as though sticking out of the dirt.

"Ernson, come over here."

The villagers had grown quiet.

"What's the matter, Stone?"

"I got black cloth in a real strange place."

Stone dug around the cloth until enough of it was worked free to grab hold of. He pulled on this, and a square of sheet metal raised its outline from the dust. The fire had been built in its center. Stone and Ernson dragged it aside and exposed the entrance to a ground tunnel.

R.W. took it upon himself to fire shots in the hole.

"R.W., back off," Ernson yelled.

"Let me go down there, Sir."

Normally, R.W. didn't have the nature to be a tunnel rat. Today he changed. Ernson gave permission for R.W. to crawl down the tunnel.

With a .45 caliber pistol in one hand and a flashlight in the other, R.W. entered.

After thirty long seconds, he called back, "There's barrels of rice and boxes of Chinese hand grenades."

After thirty more seconds, four shots were fired from deep underground.

"What the hell is it?" Ernson called.

R.W. spoke at once. "It's a girl that looks to be sixteen. She's still alive."

They waited while he dragged her up. "Take her, there's someone else in here."

Stone took hold of the girl, and R.W. went back down. The child was badly hurt. While Doc tended her, someone spied four pajama-clad gooks exiting a tunnel at the end of the village. R.W. must have flushed them out.

GIs closed in, capturing the four men. They beat the captives and dragged them before Ernson. The villagers wailed and chattered in Vietnamese.

R.W. grabbed one of the new prisoners and dragged him into a hut. Stone followed. A young woman stopped him at the entrance. She begged for the man's life, and insisted he wasn't VC.

"You fucking VC, you killed GIs!" R.W.'s hysterical accusations came from someplace hidden in his mind. "Why were you in the tunnel? Why were you in the tunnel? You kill people! You fucking kill people!"

Stone pushed the woman aside and entered in time to see R.W. smash his pistol down the side of the man's face. The woman with her children screamed from behind.

"Don't do this, R.W." Stone's words didn't sound convincing, even to his own ears. He wanted someone to suffer for what had happened to his platoon. He wanted to beat this prisoner to death.

R.W. kicked the man in the side, again and again, just like Hood had kicked the papa-san.

"Never attack your enemy in anger." Those were Asotto's words, and they came from nowhere to enter Stone's thoughts. Grabbing R.W. around the shoulders, he felt his rage. "Attention!" he yelled close to R.W.'s ear.

But R.W. kicked the gook again.

"Attention!" Stone yelled. "Attention! Attention! Attention!"

Finally, R.W. stopped, heaving like a mad dog, over the mark.

"Get a hold of yourself, soldier. Drag him outside. Get a hold of yourself," Stone said.

The woman and the children screamed and cried. The prisoner looked dead. Stone knew it was terrible, all terrible, but their grief was no greater than his own. Forty or so villagers stood in the middle of the village, mostly women and children. The Lieutenant was trying to find out why they were harboring VC.

"The Americans have been good to you, giving you food and shelter. Is this how you reward us, harboring the enemy, killing us?" R.W. screamed.

The women would say nothing. Ernson paced before them. He stopped in front of a mama, reached back as far as he could, and backhanded her across the face. Splatters of blood flew from her mouth. "You lying bitch. You're VC too."

It was all anyone could do to keep from killing the entire village.

The radio scrambled. Ernson answered, told HQ what they'd found. They were ordered to blow it up—thousands of pounds of rice, all the weapons, every home and personal possession.

Stone and the three newbies that remained in his platoon

checked each hut before torching them. In the last one, Stone pulled back the door flap to find Rabid sprawled on a grass mat. Against his leg, Rabid held a small bag of heroin. His eyes were open and glazed. He tried to raise his arm, to give Stone the peace sign.

Stone poked the barrel of the 97 against Rabid's cheek. His finger, still coated with French Fry's blood, touched the trigger. His right thumb released the safety. It would be so easy. They'd all be better off.

Rabid didn't even know the gun was there. One of the newbies entered behind Stone.

"Oh God. Don't do it, Sergeant. Let's take him back. Let Nixon kill him."

Why? Nixon doesn't give a damn about French Fry or Hagland. He could care less that Macabee didn't make it home, or Sutherland. What does it matter to President Nixon who lives and dies?

Chap licked his dry lips. They were so dry. The last hours' events had taken the living water out of his soul, and he felt like he was alone in the desert, dying of thirst.

"Come on Sarge. Let 'em put this piece of garbage in the Long Ben jail. They'll take care of his ass."

There was no good reason not to kill Rabid. He'd sold out his platoon for a lousy bag of heroin.

"You blow him away now, he'll never know what hit him. It's

too easy on him, Sarge. Let 'em lock him up without his drugs for awhile. Drag him outside."

"Yeah. Okay," he said, remembering what Mac had said that day in the mess tent: "Let him go without his heroin for a couple of days, then you'll see why they call him Rabid."

Stone pointed his gun in the air and put the safety back on. "Give me a hand. We'll take this piece of shit to the Lieutenant."

Stone reached under Rabid's left arm, the 'cruit under his right. They carried Rabid so high, his feet couldn't touch ground. Rabid was limp and heavy as French Fry had been—heavy as a man without a soul.

Ernson cursed for a full minute when he caught sight of them toting Rabid. "Found him in one of the huts, Sir." They dumped Rabid, and Stone handed the Lieutenant the bag of white powder. It was only the size of his hand.

Ernson got on the radio, and called for Medivac. "Could you stomach carrying him to the landing zone?" he asked Stone over his shoulder.

Fetching shattered VC bodies from ground pits was the easier task. Without voicing complaint, Stone carried Rabid three miles out of the jungle. He turned several times to watch the smoke rise from the burning village.

R.W. and the Lieutenant kept the prisoners in line. At the

choppers, the pilots insisted that Ernson ride along and keep an eye on his prisoner. The Lieutenant gave orders to Stone and the leader of second platoon to head back to Kootum before dark. He'd take Rabid to Long Ben and turn him over to the authorities.

### 

Entering the bunker was like entering a tomb. There was Neal's cot, Hagland's . . . French Fry's. No Macabee, no Sutherland, no Hatti, not even any damn Gonzales.

Stone looked at the tin from the fruitcake, knocked it on the floor, put the 97 to his shoulder, and fired.

"It don't mean shit." He reloaded and shot the can. "It don't mean nothin'." Reloaded and shot the can. "It don't mean shit." Reloaded and shot, "It don't . . ."

He clicked the empty chamber several more times. Doc and R.W. had entered behind him.

"Stone?" Doc put a hand on his shoulder. "You scared us, man."

Stone had never seen Doc look so pale, not even when he was hungover.

"Man, we thought it was just like Hood," R.W. said.

Stone lowered the gun. Doc slid his arm around Chap's shoulders. "By the way, the can is dead."

They erupted with laughter. When the tears came, Stone was

able to find some relief, just a little.

###

Christmas Day, Ernson called a meeting with Stone. "I have to write some letters for those guys. Is there anything you want to say? You got the day to do it."

Stone went back to his bunker and got pencil and paper. Who should he write first? Sutherland had a wife, Macabee's dad was dead, French Fry . . . he didn't know much about French Fry, and Neil . . . what could he say?

He started with French Fry. Always said he had little man's syndrome. But his courage wasn't small. Sounded pretty good. And it was true.

The afternoon passed without Stone's awareness, and he placed a little of his soul in each envelope. The letters were as much a release of pent-up rage as they were condolences to each family. When he finished, he folded each one and carried them to the Command Post bunker. Ernson wasn't there.

Top was making notations in a small ledger.

"What are you writing about?" Stone sat across from Top.

The First Sergeant clicked the top of his pen. "You, bringing these letters in here." Turning in his chair, he took a bottle of Scotch from his footlocker. "You ever stop to think that the only thing the folks back home will know about our daily existence is what we tell them?" He poured them both a drink.

That didn't seem like any great revelation. "So? Why the hell would they want to know about this hellhole?"

They drained their glasses and Top poured them another round. "Listen, I've got four kids back home. Two are in college, about to be eligible for the draft. God help them, I hope they never make it. I've been in sixteen different countries, twenty-two different states. I been away from my family for the majority of the twenty-four years I've served. Since I've been gone all that time, what do you think people would tell my children about me if I died?"

Stone held up the letters he'd just written.

"That's right. Someone else would do the telling, let them know who they thought I was." Top slung the drink down his throat and poured another. He turned back to the footlocker and lifted the lid.

"Look here, Stone. I've written hundreds of these in the last twenty years. They're just simple little log books. The same type of log book that you keep the Listening Post information in. "These little books hold my dreams. For my kids. I stayed in the Army 'cause it's the best job a black man can get. They need to know that, and no one can tell them but me. I've written my dreams . . . for my children and grandchildren. You ought to put yours down, Stone. For the ones back home."

Stone sat back in the chair, crossed his ankles. "Dreams," he laughed. "Nobody cares about what goes on over here. Your life . . . and my life don't mean shit."

"I'll tell you what, you start writing about your life, take fifteen minutes a day, and write in a book . . . , " Top scooted his chair and reached on the makeshift board and brick shelves for a clean notebook, ". . . and you might remember it means more than shit."

He handed the notebook to Stone. "Give it thirty days. If you fill it, I'll buy you a bottle of Scotch in Xuan Loc."

Stone smiled. The ordinary notebook was like a Christmas present.

He went back to the bunker and wrote his first entry. "December 25th, 1969. Dear Self, You're alive, and not insane in an insane world."

What would he think of that in thirty years? Would it still be true?

###

January 7th, 1970, more 'cruits arrived. Stone shared a pack of Marlboros with Doc and R.W. and wondered if he'd looked as young and green when he'd first come over. He didn't want the responsibility of these kids that was part of his ambivalence.

"How long will it be before they figure out not to use deodorant soap in the shower?"

Doc laughed. "I ain't telling 'em."

"I ain't either."

R.W. said laughing, "You're both cruel sons of bitches. I ain't telling 'em either."

Ernson informed them they'd be getting a full platoon in the next six days. Tet was coming. They needed to be aware of what transpired along the border.

Stone's squad and the whole company would be running LPs instead of ambushes to try and determine what Charlie was up to. The Tet of '68 had resulted in thousands of GI deaths, and the American government was scared to death it would happen again. The North Vietnamese could gather up two or three divisions and cross the Cambodian border at Kootum.

But that old threat had been hanging over Stone's head since he'd arrived. It didn't scare him anymore. Whatever came . . . came. He'd reached a place, the place he knew Hood had reached, a place where he didn't hear the voice of limitations anymore, where the only thing that mattered was what he chose to do. He was deep in the world of brashness, he guessed. His mother didn't plead with him, nor did his conscience, and damn sure not God. He called the shots. It was a place beyond fear.

Yet, it wasn't the only thing inside of him. He knew that now, since seeing French Fry's death. Inside was still something human. He couldn't afford to feel it every day, but he knew it was there. It hadn't been annihilated by himself or by Vietnam.

Maybe it was the mercy of God, on ice like the beer Ellie put in the Meramac cooler.

Maybe it was a refusal to die.

# KOOTUM, VIETNAM, 1970
## CHAP STONE
### CHAPTER 11

> "We're all Isaac here, just laying it down for the good old USA."
>
> —Chap Stone

Stone poured a thin line of hot wax along the seam of his pants, the next best thing to starch in the jungle. He'd make sure the mama-san pressed every wrinkle out of his clothes.

While he waited, Chap shined his boots until they shone like black water. Once dressed, he pulled the hat tight on his well-shaven head.

It was mid-January, and he dodged puddles on the way to the Company Commander's bunker. The humidity was so high, it felt like he could catch water in his cupped hands and wet his dry throat.

In the bunker, Top whistled over Stone's appearance. He let him in to see the captain.

Collins was less impressed. "What's with all this formal shit?" He motioned Stone to sit on the single folding chair.

"Sir, I have a request. I respectfully ask permission to take the newbies on an ambush, Sir."

The CO stood, grabbed an ink pen and rolled it between his hands. "You want to make this war personal. That's what you're telling me, Sergeant."

"Sir, I feel we need to do this for the guys who lost their lives during a damn cease-fire."

The CO snapped the pen. "Stand up and come to attention."

Stone did as ordered. Collins rounded the desk and got in his face. "You do not kill in anger. You do not kill out of your own frustrations. In fact, you never kill. You only follow orders. Do you understand, Sergeant?"

Stone didn't respond.

"Vietnam is only an action taken by our government. You are nothing more than its representative. This is not Sergeant Chap Stone's private war. Do you understand?"

Stone understood, but he couldn't make his mouth say the words.

The CO backed off. "At ease." He yanked out his chair and sat down.

"What the hell did they die for?" Stone bit his lip to keep it from trembling.

Collins stared at him for a long time. "They died honorably. They died defending what their country believes."

Stone thought to himself, *What if you didn't agree with your* country? Did you still owe them your life? Is that what allegiance to the flag and patriotism was—blind faith?

"Sit down, Stone. Sit the hell down."

He dropped to the chair.

"You know what we do here, soldier? Bottom line? We lay it down. We lay it down every damn day, every damn minute. Some of us make it, some of us don't. But we go on laying it down because that's what we do. Those men out there laid it down for us, and we honor them by carrying on. Day in. Day out. Every hour and minute of the day, no matter how we feel, inside, outside. We suck it up and lay it down.

"I think it's time you took one more step toward being a full-fledged platoon sergeant. We have new orders for this company. Tet is just a few weeks away. In all likelihood, this will be the point of the border the NVA will cross. Our company has been selected to implement the new Vietnamization Policy. We'll start doing less of the fighting and let the South Vietnamese do more. What this also means is we'll start teaching them to fight. You'll take into your platoon Sergeant Nien Beat. I put him with you because he's had airborne training. Figured you'd have something in common."

Something in common with a gook? "I don't like gooks, Sir."

"You are ordered to like this one. The President says so. Sergeant Beat will have several men under his command. You'll instruct him in everything you know, and he'll interpret for you."

"Yes, Sir."

"Go on and get out of here. You're making the rest of us look like shit in those starched fatigues."

### 

Before Stone exited the hootch, Top laid out plans for the compound and explained how they were going to reinforce with sandbags. Stone would lead the detail.

Much as he hated laterite dust, the miserable sandbagging would bring welcome relief from the tedium, and the grief. In his bunker, Stone took off the starched fatigues and dressed down. At Doc's, he told the story of his ridiculous visit to Collins. They shared a beer and a laugh.

A few minutes later, R.W. appeared, holding a multipaged letter and looking sick. "What's the matter with you?" Doc asked.

R.W. plopped onto one of the cots and let the paper float to the ground. "It's my dad. He's had a stroke. He's not going to live much longer. Mom said they went to the Red Cross, and I'm getting emergency leave to go home."

"That's a hell of a raw deal," Doc sympathized. "I wish you were going home under better conditions, but who knows, they might let you serve stateside until your time is out."

For a full minute they sat in silence.

"I hope I can make it home before he dies."

"Maybe he'll pull through," Stone said.

"I don't think so. Everything's changing."

###

The next morning, Stone called for formation in front of the CP hootch. It was only sunrise, and the heat hadn't taken impact yet. They had a new leader, a Lieutenant Saborn. Ernson had been transferred to another unit.

Stone turned the platoon over to the Lieutenant. Saborn wore tailored fatigues right out of Brooks Brothers, and claimed to be a West Point graduate. He had a square jaw, no moustache, and was freshly shaved with a military haircut.

He called them to attention and gave the morning's orders. "Today you will begin strengthening our position by filling sandbags. These will be placed over your bunkers and around the perimeter."

It was only a matter of time before Saborn noticed Spock, a newbie from another squad. Spock hadn't mastered the basics, rarely stood at attention, wore a headband instead of a hat, a peace symbol around his neck, and was always high. If Spock was in Stone's squad, someone would probably have killed him after what they'd been through with Rabid. But Spock was oblivious of Saborn's glare, or Saborn's boots eating the ground between them.

The Lieutenant got in Spock's face and blasted him with a voice like a bull horn. Any normal human being would have snapped to attention, but Spock didn't react.

"Soldier," Saborn screamed, "do you hear me?"

Spock smiled, twisted the plug out of his ear, reached in his pocket and turned off his transistor. "No man, but I can now."

Saborn spat on the ground, close to Spock's unlaced boots. "Attention, you dumb-ass piece of hippie shit."

Spock came to attention, a model of army protocol—if Saborn wanted to ignore his uniform and shaggy hair.

He didn't. The Lieutenant shouted a list of Spock's sins, then returned to pace before Stone's men.

Spock's "Wow, man, where'd he come from?" reached everyone's ears, and bursts of laughter broke throughout formation. With his face a high red, Saborn continued to inform them about the new Vietnamization Policy. When he was finished, a newbie in the back raised his hand.

"What is it, Soldier?"

"Sir, Hanoi Hannah says we're supposed to love the gooks. If that's the case, Sir, I need to go out and hug me a whore."

Again, the platoon broke into laughter. A couple of the men bent all the way forward, they laughed so hard.

Saborn didn't appreciate the joke. "Attention."

They snapped to attention, muffled laughter still breaking out along the line.

"Sergeant Stone, please take your platoon out of the compound to the laterite pit and begin your detail. Bring back as many sandbags as you can."

These new shitheads had pissed the Lieutenant off and now they'd be working in the hot sun all day, learning the hard way.

###

Laterite was a red clay soil. Dry, it was a miserable, skin-blistering dust; wet, it was sticky enough to be used for pottery.

Stone wanted to stay out of the stuff and let the newbies handle this job.

He had the men set up a safety perimeter. Charlie had been shelling them regularly again. Getting ambushed was not on Stone's menu for the day.

He watched the newbies filling the bags. For days he'd ignored them, happy when they staggered around sick from their induction, daring any of them to waste his time with small talk. But watching them toil in the hot sun, Stone was finally softening enough to ask a couple of them their names.

The man closest was a big, square-built guy, a Swede. He told Stone his name was Sergeant Major. It was said with such good nature, Stone could only chuckle.

"How'd you end up over here?"

"I volunteered, Sergeant, soon as I graduated high school. My daddy was in World War II, and I planned on killing me some gooks."

The fellow working next to Sergeant Major looked like Sergeant Rock out of the cartoon book. He had a powerful jaw, a barrel chest, and blond hair. He'd been the one to talk Stone out of shooting Rabid, and Stone hadn't acknowledged it, didn't want the connection, didn't want to like him, or know him well.

"My friends call me Even," the guy volunteered. "Say I'm the most even-tempered man they ever met."

He stepped forward and shook Stone's hand, grinding dust between their palms.

"We've met."

"Yes Sergeant."

"I didn't tell you then . . . thanks."

"No problem. I wanted to kill him too, and I wasn't even as close to the guys who died as you were."

Stone didn't want to talk about that day, didn't want to think about Rabid. "Yeah, well, get back to work. We've got a lot of bags to fill before sundown."

The platoon had toiled most of the day. They'd filled a two-and-a-half-ton truck and were working on filling an extra trailer. Lieutenant Saborn rode to the pit in a jeep. Stone knew he wanted to make sure the men were doing the job. He had a completely different style of leadership than Ernson. Ernson befriended and had won the men over, but could be hard when he had to. Saborn was just hard.

He inspected the perimeter and complimented Stone for doing it right. "Lieutenant, what's this Vietnamization mean to us, anyway? Does it mean we're going home?" Even asked.

The men weren't going to let it rest. They had Saborn on the run and knew it.

"Nixon thinks the best way to get out of Nam is to turn this war over to the gooks and let them settle it."

"Does that mean we lost this war?" Sergeant Major asked.

Saborn shifted his feet, took a wide-legged stance. "No, we've not lost the war. It's in our best interest to turn this thing over and get out gradually."

Sergeant Major said, "Sounds like losing to me."

"Who cares, man? Gooks are gooks. Let them have this sorry place. Send my ass home," Spock voiced a rare opinion.

Saborn looked bewildered by the attitude of the men. "Vietnamization is a way to step out of here with grace and dignity."

Sergeant Major leaned on his shovel and scratched the back of his neck. "How can you lose with grace and dignity?"

Saborn's knees jerked, first the left, then the right. He set his jaw, and the high, red color in his cheeks wasn't all from the sun.

Stone knew the lieutenant needed help, and knew he needed to learn from his own mistakes. Anyway, he'd been in the army long enough to know officers didn't come out on the short end of the stick. "Sir, we gotta have two hundred more bags before this evening. Could we carry on this discussion later?"

"Sure thing, Sergeant. You men get back to work."

Stone walked Saborn to the jeep.

"There is one good thing about Vietnamization, Sergeant. We'll start getting gooks in our company tomorrow. It'll be our job to teach them to fight."

One of the 'cruits overheard. "Sir, does that mean we have to eat rice balls for dinner?" Everyone cracked a snicker.

The Lieutenant jumped in, working a muscle in his jaw as he glared at the men. "See that they get those two hundred bags filled, Stone. I don't care if they have to work in the dark."

### 

Early February, 1970. Stone's day was filled with training the ARVNs. These men had been drafted into the South Vietnamese Army. They were given uniforms, M16s, bayonets, and backpacks. But they had absolutely no military skills.

Most of the men felt like Stone. They'd rather do the fighting themselves than teach these guys. A sorrier bunch of fighting men had never been assembled.

Usually soldiers had a fire in their bellies that could be kindled for battle. These men didn't seem to have that. The first time trouble showed it face, Stone worried that any Vietnamese they took with them would run.

Their ability with weapons was so poor, they'd be better off putting the gun on automatic and hoping for a hit. Worst of all, the Americans shared an underlying fear that any number of these new 'cruits were really Charlie Cong.

Charlie was North Vietnamese Army (NVA). Charlie Cong was NVA who pretended to be South Vietnamese. He was a traitor. Judging the accuracy of Charlie's mortar attacks from across the Cambodian border, Charlie Cong did his job very well.
Yet, in spite of this ever-present fear of betrayal, Stone picked up some of their language and got to know them. Slowly, many of the ARVNs were becoming friends.

The rebellious attitudes Saborn's arrival had exposed continued to change. Vietnamization heightened the GIs' indifference toward winning the war and just wanting to survive and go home.

Kootum was a fortress, where ARVNs and GIs waited for Charlie. But other than periodic mortar attacks, Charlie didn't come.

# KOOTUM, VIETNAM 1970
# CHAP STONE
# CHAPTER 12

> "If a man's life is worth living, it ought to be worth recording."
>
> —First Sergeant Top

It was quiet in the jungle. The hard training of the last weeks had paid off. The platoon followed every order exactly. Doc walked about a hundred meters back, but Stone wished he was closer. At least R.W. made it out of Nam for a while. He should be home in the states, saying goodbye to his dad.

By suppertime, they still hadn't engaged the enemy. Their orders were to stay put and eat a cold meal until reconnaissance returned.

The men set up a perimeter, the usual defenses, and an LP. Saborn made radio contact with a squad twenty-five kilometers north who'd taken heavy casualties. Stone was grateful for every second they weren't yet in the fight.

He went to each group of men and reviewed their mission. This was Nixon's Fishhook Plan—seventy thousand GIs crossing the Cambodian border to attempt a rescue some one hundred POWs.

During training, even the most lethargic had come to life—

heads, juicers, volunteers, and draftees, even short-timers wanted the chance to liberate the prisoners of war.

All that first night, they kept vigil. Stone wished he could walk point, but had too many responsibilities. By noon of the second day, reconnaissance returned. They found a camp where prisoners were held. When asked how it was fortified, the recon man, R.J., made eye contact with Saborn.

"Two Russian tanks."

"Oh shit," Saborn said. They'd hoped to find less resistance.

R.J. drew a quick map in the sand for the two lieutenants and platoon sergeants. The camp was only half a mile away. There were four towers, manned by Charlie.

Several troop trucks were in the compound. They watched the tanks move back and forth for over an hour, but couldn't see any POWs. Of course, they would be in the huts. Each was guarded by NVA regulars, not just Charlies.

Saborn radioed the CO. Collins was on his way with reinforcements. They were ordered to wait in place. He'd be there in two hours.

The captain arrived at 1630 hrs., giving them a force of two hundred and fifty men. Collins studied the plans Saborn laid out, and agreed that they had to make a three-pronged approach.

The river protected them from behind. One group would go to

the west and two would take up positions in front. They had the RPGs and the LAWs to handle the tanks and towers.

Roughly seventy-five men were designated to carry out the most serious POW casualties. Hopefully, the others would be able to walk.

As they entered the jungle, every noise was kept to a minimum. Less than a quarter mile from the camp, Captain Collins ordered them to sit in place and wait until dark.

Four reconnaissance men were sent in to check the area. They were given specific orders not to engage in contact for any reason. At nine-thirty that night, they returned, reporting that other than some movement by one of the trucks, everything, including the tanks, was still.

Around midnight, the captain ordered them to move in slowly and get into position. Stone could see the compound. Either everyone was asleep or it was deserted.

His orders were to take out the towers, beginning with the one on the southwest corner.

Four streaks of light flashed across the sky. The first tower became a smoldering stub. As the LAWs exploded the rest of the towers, their red tracers cut across the tanks. There was no response.

Starting with Collins, the hand signals were quickly passed to cease fire. The captain ordered them to move in slowly. Stone was more afraid of tripwires and landmines than he was of the enemy shooting him. He hoped the rest of his platoon was too.

The Russian tank was beneath a smoking tower. Crawling near, Stone heard the radio playing from the open top hatch. Oh, shit, I'm gonna wet my pants.

He felt for a grenade, popped the pin, and held the lever with his sweaty thumb.

Climbing over the rear engine department, he felt the warmth from recent movement. He crept toward Hanoi Hannah's voice.

"Your people are killing your students today," she said. "In America, on your college campuses, your terroristic soldiers are killing your kids just like you're killing ours."

He inched closer to the top, wanting a look inside before he launched the grenade.

"On your college campuses in Ohio," Hannah continued, "your soldiers are killing students. Massacring them by the thousands."

Stone inched forward, looked in the tank. No one was there.

The GIs swept the rest of the village. Nothing was found but several old ammunition boxes filled with documents. These were stacked by a blazing fire.

Even asked Stone, "Can I take a look at that stuff?"

"Leave that shit. Don't touch it."

"It could be important, Sergeant."

"I said leave it. Check out the rest of the compound."

Stone took a look in the first hootch. In the corner was a pile of human feces and short pieces of rope for tying hands and feet. It was like that in the next hootch, and the next.

A rice paddy was in the center of the compound. Bamboo cages stood in the water, submerged enough to make a man stand thigh deep in the cold water. Stone imagined a pilot locked in one of these for days, a feast for the mosquitoes and leeches, knowing if he fell asleep too many times, he would drown.

Far into the compound was a wooden cage loaded onto an oxcart. Blood had caked and dried on its bars and floor. Stone asked Sergeant Bien to translate the sign tacked on its bars.

" 'These men are the killers of your children. They burned your homes. You may hate them,'" Bien read. "They parade these men through villages that have been bombed. Villagers stick and poke, hurt men in the cages."

Stone wanted to torch this place. He knelt to study the tracks near the hootches. The tracks weren't dry. It looked like they'd evacuated about an hour before. When the first recon man had made his report of activity in the compound, they must have been loading the POWs to get out.

Somehow Charlie knew. He didn't want to suspect the ARVNs. They'd proved as loyal as any man in the squad. But the uncertainty would always be there.

The compound was checked and rechecked. There were no weapons, nothing of value, just the boxes of documents by the fire.

"Should we get those papers?" Saborn asked.

"No," Stone said. "Leave them in place."

Ten minutes later, Stone was rounding up the men when he heard the explosion. He ran to the fire. Someone said it was Even. He'd picked up one of the boxes and a mine went off. Saborn had given the order.

There wasn't much left of Even. Stone grabbed his tags and handed them to the Lieutenant. He commandeered a couple of poles from the bamboo pit, and with Sergeant Major's help they strung a poncho between them. They transferred Even's body to their homemade stretcher.

In than sixty minutes, the mission had failed, and with heavy hearts; the Lieutenant ordered them back in a column as they pulled out.

The Russian T-76 tanks were filled with enough artillery to blow them all home. They'd put a delayed satchel charge in each one. When the tanks blew, Stone felt a healthy kick of satisfaction. *Name's Even. Most even-tempered man . . .*

"It don't mean nothin'. It don't mean nothin'. But God, God . . . I know it does," thought Stone.

Stone turned his end of the stretcher over to one of the newbies. *It's Saborn's fault. Oh hell, what does it matter? It's the gooks. No, no, Collins said it's not my private war. It's a government action carried out by the military, and that's me. So it doesn't matter. None of it matters because I'm a fucking robot.*

They stopped in a clearing and set up camp. Stone heard over the radio that another squad found the control center and taken a lot of casualties, but the center was also vacant.

The Hueys were going to pull them out as soon as daylight broke.

### 

It was 0530 hrs. when the first tripflare went off.

Stone had an ugly feeling inside as he walked by each man telling him to dig in a little farther. He found Doc and checked that he was in a safe position. Three minutes later, a second tripflare signaled. Two dozen had been set out. Stone wished they'd set out as many claymores instead.

One minute more, two flares shot off almost simultaneously. The enemy was circling at a three-sixty.

"Will Saborn be able to order artillery with Charlie this close?" Doc asked.

"Hell no. That's Charlie's trick," Stone told Doc. "He gets in so close, he grabs you by the damn belt buckle. You can't blow him away;

you've got to practically shoot him in the nose. I better get over there. Saborn's about to get an education. Take care of yourself."

"Yeah," Doc whispered. "You too."

Stone could see the fear on Doc's face and wished he could make it better somehow. "Not possible today," he told himself.

Stone was halfway to the Lieutenant, when their whole world exploded.

# CAMBODIAN BORDER, 1970
# ROGER "DOC" MURPHY
# CHAPTER 13

> "Greater love hath no man than this, that a man lay down his life for his friends."
>
> —John 15:13

Doc watched as incoming hit less than ten meters away from Stone. Stone's face was twisted as he rose in the air and fell to the earth. Landing on his back with a thud that could be heard above the shells. Stone clenched his teeth in pain but did not utter a sound.

"Incoming, incoming, incoming," several voices yelled at once.

Stone was dead. No one could survive a blast like that and live.

Someone yanked Doc to the ground. Incoming traveled through the earth, rattling his bones.

Chap's dead. Chap's dead. He's dead.

There was no time to think. They'd taken heavy casualties. As Doc worked to stop arterial bleeding, to bandage, or check a pulse, he thanked God that R.W. was in the states.

The NVA attacked in waves. Even without a platoon sergeant,

Saborn held them together. For every casualty Saborn's men took, they inflicted ten.

At full daylight, Collins was finally able to get on the radio. The airwaves were jammed with other voices as urgent as his own.

"Shut the fuck up," Collins yelled, "and get off the radio!" The CO gave the position and marked it with smoke. Then the Cobras came in and strafed just meters away.

Finally, Charlie withdrew.

Doc had never treated so many wounded. He quit counting at seventeen. All four medics worked relentlessly. Yet, more died than not.

From where he worked over a GI's flayed cheek, Doc could see the triage area. He laid strips of flesh over the wound, and his glance went to the thirty-seven bodies laying in a row, covered with poncho liners.

Stone, a lump covered in plastic, two feet sticking out, or maybe just one. *Not Chap.*

The Hueys began to land. They took the most severely wounded out first. For the rest of the day, Doc tended those who must wait their turn. He was exhausted, but couldn't have rested in a downy four-poster bed in the quietest town in the states. Not with the load of grief he carried.

He was growing clumsy . . . all thumbs, distracted. The activity was a blessing, yet he cursed it.

At the end of the day Doc came face to face with Saborn. Too bad Chap couldn't have seen how the Lieutenant had performed. He earned that Brooks Brothers suit.

"Lieutenant, about Stone . . . did he make it?" Doc didn't want this answer, but had to know for sure.

"I checked with the pilot. He didn't have a chance," Saborn said.

Doc took faltering steps to a nearby tree. He pulled his helmet off and slid against the trunk to the ground. Was that really the same sky that covered Hillsboro, Illinois? Was that the same sun, shining on his family in turn? He'd believed in its warmth once. What did he believe in now?

He was alone. God, he hated being alone. He'd do anything not to be alone.

Nothing made sense. Not life. Not death. Nothing.

"I can't find you, God," he whispered, banging the back of his head against the tree. "I can't find you; I can't find you."

### 

Doc returned to Kootum on May 8th. The first thing he did was write R.W. and let him know about Stone. He told R.W. how they'd tried to get the POWs out and that they walked into an ambush.

He closed with a warning. "If I was in your shoes, R.W., I

wouldn't come back. I mean it, buddy. If you can see your way, don't come back here."

Doc sealed the flap and wrote, "Free" on the right-hand corner. He took it to the CO's bunker where the mail went out. Top spotted him.

"I was just sending someone to get you. CO wants to see you. Buck up a little bit, it might be good news."

Collins looked grave. "Seems you're not wanted, soldier. The Army has enough medics in Nam. You're a three-day wonder. Looks like you're going home."

"Run that by me again, CO?"

"We're sending you back to the Ninetieth. You should be home any day."

And he'd said he couldn't find God.

###

Doc didn't want to take anything home from Vietnam other than a few photos he put in a box and mailed ahead.

As promised, he was in Long Ben just two days later, taking his first real shower in months. The hot water flushed the red clay from his skin. He thanked God it was just his suntan running down the drain and not his blood.

At the end of the second day, Doc had another physical.

"Anything really wrong with you?" the doctor asked when he

finished the exam.

"Would that be with my body or my head?"

"Your body, soldier. I don't want to hear about the rest."

Doc woke early the third morning. There were three hours to kill before they shipped him out. To alleviate the boredom, he stuck his hands deep in his pockets and strolled around the village. At the far end of the road, a chaplain spoke to a group of some fifty new recruits. Curiosity drew Doc.

The Chaplain should be talking to the guys going home. We're the ones who need some answers—answers he probably doesn't have.

He thought about Stone, saw him thrown into the air for the hundredth time. His thoughts turned to Nixon and his failed Fishhook plan to get the POWs out of Cambodia; of Even dying over a box of papers . . . of Hood, Spock, Sergeant Major, Neil, Macabee, and all the others who'd fried and died.

The 'cruits seemed to hang on the Chaplain's every word. Doc got close enough to hear. "Vietnam is not a never-ending war. You must have a belief in our leaders, that they are doing this to end Communism," the Chaplain said.

"You idiot."

Several turned their heads to look at Doc, but the Chaplain continued, "Yes, our men in the armed forces are taking casualties, but we're killing over five hundred NVA every day, too. We're making progress."

"Sir," Doc called, pushing near the front of the group, "how can a man of the cloth look at their faces and tell them that bullshit? Why don't you guys try the truth for a change? You remember that, right? Some of these guys are going to die. They're all going to lose good friends. A few will be maimed, and even if they're lucky enough to leave in one piece, like me, they won't ever be the same. So quit telling them your holy bullshit. When their whole world blows up in their faces, how are they going to handle it? You're selling the government and you're selling God, and from what I've seen, one don't have anything to do with the other. When they leave this place, it's not operation Fishhook, or Nixon's Vietnamization, or any of the other bullshit government actions they'll remember. It'll be a buddy sharing a Ballantine on the berm, listening to you cry because your dad is dying and you want to go home. Or the orphanages where they tried to patch up some of these kids this war has left without parents. They'll get there hearts broken here. There's some heavy shit. But they'll see some good things, too. In a way . . . the best of themselves."

Doc ran a hand through his hair. "I've got a plane to catch."

The crowd parted to let him pass. He wasn't out of earshot when the Chaplain continued, "President Nixon's Vietnamization plan is working and will get us home soon and safely."

### 

They rode the bus to the airfield. Two hundred thirty of them boarded the waiting Pan Am airplane. Doc was just calming down from his speech. He felt tired and drained, and he didn't know where those words had come from, didn't know they were inside of him, or how he'd really felt until he'd framed his thoughts and spoken them aloud. He believed. He had faith. Maybe he even had hope. But it wasn't the kind you could find in a book. It was real, this hope. It was a hope that maybe . . . he could be stronger than all the crap in the world, all the death, all the unfairness; hope that he could choose somewhere in himself to say there is something more. If war could cause so much pain and loss, then couldn't a life of helping people through medicine create a world where he could heal?

It made him cry. He could cry buckets of tears now as the fear left him. He was glad he could feel this pain inside, this life inside, because dead people couldn't feel at all.

As they filed patiently onto the plane wearing new khaki uniforms, Doc thought it was odd how most of them carried nothing. They had brought too much here, too much for this place. Now they were going home with broken hearts and empty hands; but full inside, full of turmoil, pain, ghosts and memories, but alive.

Doc got a seat near the rear. As the men settled into their seats, there was laughter and small talk—remember this town, this whore, this soda girl, this trinket . . .

It was so hot that each breath felt like you were taking air in that was heated in an oven. Suddenly the air came rushing through the small overhead vents and they buckled their seat belts. Doc closed his eyes. Immediately, he saw Stone flying through the air. That was okay. He knew better than to fight the image. It was a part of him now.

The door closed and the stewardess clicked the emergency lever. The engine roared. They jerked into movement. There was a vacuum of silence. They looked at each other, but the silence grew, until it pressed each man into his seat.

The plane clicked across the asphalt bumps, but they couldn't hear it, they were deep in the vacuum now, waiting . . . waiting.

This silence was greater than the roar of the engines. The scenery passed faster and faster. The $g$ force pushed them firmly against the backs of their chairs. Still, there was only silence.

Leaving the ground, the plane's ascent was unbroken. As it leveled out, roars of laughter and cheering shattered the silence. "God, we made it."

Doc let it go. Tears ran down his cheeks, and he swallowed hard. More tears came, his lips parted, and his face scrunched into an emotional fist.

The stewardesses came down the aisle, shaking hands, hugging. They cried, too.
One hugged Doc. She was as old as his mom but still pretty. "It's this way every time we go home," she said.

It was a wonderful trip all the way back. It seemed like they landed at Travis Air Force Base, in Fairfield, California, in no time.

As soon as they opened the plane's door, Doc noticed the difference in the air—cool and misty. He could smell the ocean.

They exited onto a stairway, about a hundred yards from the terminal. Doc was one of the last ones to disembark. He slid his hand along the cool metal banister saying a silent prayer of thanks that his feet were touching American ground.

To the far right, at the cargo area of the plane, he noticed the men from burial details unloading black body bags.

"Chap." Of course, he'd been on the plane, too.

Doc walked closer to the tail. He raised his hand in a salute, and held that position until the last bag had been removed.

Then he stood alone, the sea breeze caressing his face, drying each new tear that rolled down his cheeks.

He thought of his friend, the big old country boy from Neosho. Chap hadn't known there were days when Doc had thought, *If I can just see Chap, everything will be all right.*

Chap had tried so hard to do his duty, but inside he was gentle. Doc always knew that; he'd sensed it from the beginning. That was what had drawn them to one another. That was where they'd been alike.

He wanted to tell himself it didn't "mean nothing" and walk

on. But the time for lies was over. It meant everything—knowing Chap and losing him. It meant everything.

He'd keep in touch with R.W. For himself and Chap. Even if it was only a Christmas card, somehow he'd keep in touch. The loss would stop today.

# RONALD WILKENS
# KENT, OHIO
# CHAPTER 14

> "Those who profess to favor freedom, and yet depreciate agitation, are men who want rain without thunder and lightning. They want the ocean without the roar of its many waters."
>
> —Frederick Douglass

R.W. finally arrived at the Cincinnati airport April 9th, 1970. His mother and sister anxiously waited for him. Mom had aged. Her hair was completely gray. Had he been gone that long, or was it Dad's illness that had taken such a toll? He wondered as he hugged her for a long time.

Erma's appearance also jarred him. She was a senior in high school, full-blown beautiful—long dark hair, silky white skin, and a micro-mini skirt to go with it.

R.W. wanted to tell her she was swell, but wasn't sure how to compliment his sister. "How's dad?"

"He's still here. C'mon, let's get your bag and go home. It's a long drive."

Being from a college town, R.W. was well acquainted with

hippie attire. But it seemed to him that hippies were everywhere; men with hair hanging below their shoulders, wearing bell-bottomed pants the size of some women's skirts, earrings in their ears, and long moustaches. Most of them looked like a good bath wouldn't hurt.

"Isn't it exciting?" Erma asked when they reached the unusual bustle of Kent.

"What the heck's going on around here?" he asked.

"It's the students," Mom said. "I tell you, we got Communists running that campus. Your daddy was so upset about it, R.W. Sometimes I think they're to blame for his stroke. If he wasn't carrying on about the Vietnam War, he was raving about the students."

"Oh, Mom. They're not Communists," Erma said, then to R.W., "Kent State's been the scene of students protesting the war. Our journalism department from the high school has been taking pictures. The big news people have been sending crews here. It's so exciting."

"Don't tell me my own sister's been protesting the war while I've been over there getting my butt shot at for my country."

"Now don't be like Daddy, R.W.," Erma folded her arms and bounced her shoulders against the back seat.

"Well, I've had all the excitement I care to handle for a while. I came home for some peace and quiet, not to find out my sister's turned into a hippie."

Erma pouted the rest of the way home. R.W. tried to ignore

her. When they reached the house, he got his bag out of the back of Dad's '63 Pontiac station wagon and looked at the place.

How many times he'd thought of this house, and now he stood before it. It was smaller than he'd remembered. Nothing fancy really, but home. His home.

"Hey, Erma, I didn't mean to be hard. It's just . . . people are dying over there."

"That's why they're protesting, Ronnie. It's wrong."

"I don't want to argue. Come here and give me a hug."

He put his arms around her. She smelled sweet, and it tugged at his heart to realize how innocent she was . . . how clean.

"McGovern's going to give a big speech in a few days at the campus, and Jane Fonda is coming."

"We'll talk about it later."

In the house, he took a quick look at his room.

"Are you hungry, R.W.?"

"What have you got, Mom?"

She had chicken and potato salad, baked beans, coleslaw, cornbread, and chocolate cake. He ate like a liberated refugee.

"Don't take your uniform off, R.W. I want Dad to see it."

After dinner, R.W. and his mom drove to Kent's small hospital.

On the way, mom repeated what she'd already written when he

was in Nam.

"Pop started getting headaches around Christmas that never went away. Things got tough at the mill. I told him, he should've taken night classes like some of the others. When big promotions came along, those were the fellas that got them. But he didn't want to go back to school. I don't know. I found him slumped over his workbench in the garage. They said he had a stroke. He's opened his eyes a couple of times, but he doesn't recognize me. The doctor thinks he's had a couple of what they call 'mini-strokes' since then."

"What's going to happen to him? Do they think there's any hope?"

She flapped her hand. "He's dying, son. Just like I said in the letter."

R.W. had tried to prepare himself, but it was worse hearing it from her lips.

"You know, son, your father would be so proud of you. You look just like him when he came home from World War II. He talked about you all the time. Everyone knew his son served in Vietnam. Not like these young kids at the college causing all this trouble. I'm so grateful to have a son like you."

R.W. saw himself beating the Vietnamese man in front of his screaming wife and children. He felt the terrible darkness in the tunnel, and the horror of shooting the little girl.

Maybe Mom was proud, but that was only because she was ignorant. She didn't know him as he was, didn't know his sins, what he'd been willing to do to survive.

Walking into the hospital, the antiseptic smells heightened R.W.'s dread. He grabbed the Garrison cap off his head and pulled it through his belt.

Had he always towered over his mother? He wasn't a tall man by any standards, but he kept his shoulders square and carried himself straight. Mom seemed to be shrinking.

"It's right down here," Mom pointed at the last open door. Maybe if he could look at R.W. and recognize him, things would be all right, she thought.

There wasn't much in the room. Dad was on the bed, his normally full-term belly looking sunken beneath the covers. He looked like a skeleton in a body bag of skin.

"He's lost a little weight." Mom's voice sounded like an explosion in this quiet place.

"They got every gadget and gizmo in the joint hooked up to him."

"That's what we want, Mom. We want them to do all they can."

R.W. walked to the other side of the bed and touched his father's hand. He bent over and kissed him on the cheek, tried to remember if he'd done that before.

"I . . . I gotta find the nurse," his mother stammered bolting from the room.

He was glad she left. He whispered in Dad's ear, "I'm home. Daddy, I'm home," as if those words could raise Lazarus.

They didn't have any effect on his father. R.W. had seen the look of death enough times to know he was too late.

It was dusk by the time Mom told him they needed to leave. He'd sat hunched in the aqua-colored vinyl armchair, rubbing Dad's arm for hours.

She blustered around the room, moving the chairs back along the wall and watering Dad's one plant.

R.W. shrugged into his coat. Before leaving he unpinned his combat/infantry badge and pinned it to his father's pillow. Mom's soft cries didn't stop him from taking his time, from bending to kiss Dad good-bye.

Minutes later, as they walked down the hall, Mom said, "Your father saw what you did in there, R.W. He knew, and he's so proud."

Funny how she felt it her duty to soften things for him, just like when he was a kid. "We're both proud. Even Erma . . . she's proud too, R.W. All that nonsense about the protests. She's just a child."

*Are you proud of me? Did you know I shot a girl in Vietnam? Just a kid, younger than Erma. Do you know I beat a man in front of his wife and kids? He probably died. That's how badly I beat him. But it don't mean nothing,* he told himself, and that was the first severe wave of confusion.

What didn't mean nothing? Dad dying?

No, he thought fiercely. The gooks . . . Vietnam . . . they don't mean nothing. The thoughts rolled like a snowball downhill in R.W.'s mind.

Yeah. The gooks. But over here they call them the Vietnamese people. North Vietnamese or South Vietnamese, not Charlie, not Charlie Cong, and never, ever gooks.

He'd approach this the military way, set up a perimeter around Vietnam and all the things his family could never understand. Inside that perimeter nothing would matter. Outside, everything would be like it was—home, Mom, Dad, Erma. Outside the perimeter was where he really lived. Inside, that was his other life, the one that must be contained, the one where nothing mattered.

But what about Stone and Doc? Didn't they matter?

Of course they did. Of course.

He opened his mother's car door and waited while she got in. He couldn't think right now. Maybe later he'd straighten it all out. There had to be a way. But right now, he couldn't think.

### 

The ringing phone brought R. W. out of a terrible dream. He woke up sweating and panting, with the feeling he'd been hearing explosions and running for his life. His bedroom door creaked open. Erma stood there in a full, white nightgown looking like an angel.

"Daddy died. Mom just hung up the phone, and she won't talk."

"Go on and sit with her. I'll . . . be right there."

He licked his dry lips and tried to swallow. So many times he'd had to deal with sudden terror, and this was no different. Everything inside of him wanted to run. He didn't want to face his mother, tell her everything would be all right when they all knew it wouldn't.

Quickly, he went to his bag in the closet, dug around until he felt the chunky bottle of Jim Beam. He unscrewed the cap and took a long drink. Then another. If he held out his hand, it trembled like a man with Parkinson's disease. He took one more swig before going out to face his mom.

### 

Monday evening, Erma was scheduled to sing in her school play. She'd practiced for weeks, but wanted to cancel. "I can't go ahead with it now that Daddy's died."

But Mom wouldn't hear of her canceling. "He'd want you to go ahead, Kitten, you know he would."

"Would you come too, R.W.?"

"Of course he'll come," Mom answered for him. "He'll be there for Daddy."

That morning, while Erma was at church, Mom asked him to help pick out Dad's burial clothes. He followed her to the bedroom, watched as she bustled about doing it herself.

When Mom's back was turned, R.W. added a hefty swig of Jim Beam to his orange juice. Then he ate Mom's scrambled eggs and bacon. "Mom, you didn't have to do all this. I'm sure you must feel tired."

"Nonsense. I got to keep busy."

He knew how she could drive a person insane when she was like this. It would be nonstop, incessant activity until they'd want to shut her in the basement.

By mid-morning, he took her to the funeral home to pick out the casket and make the arrangements. She picked a big silver box that reminded R.W. of a refrigerator.

At home, she cleaned out the real refrigerator and heated most of the leftovers for R.W.'s lunch. He sat in Dad's easy chair before the television, cramming forkfuls of food down his dry throat and reading the Sunday paper.

The paper had given the Vietnam casualty count for the second week of April 1970. Four hundred seventy-one died, with eight hundred ten wounded. They also reported that on average the NVA losses were ten times as high as ours.

"Shit," he said under his breath.

In the background, R.W. heard Mom on the phone, calling the relatives about Dad's death. A couple of times she reiterated, "No, Ronald SENIOR passed away."

R.W. realized some were thinking he died instead.

Every time Mom called another relative or friend, at exactly the same place in her spiel, right between, "Dorothy (or Fred, or Ginny), I've got terrible news. Ronald passed a . . . (huge gush of tears) . . . way."

Damn. I've got to get out of here, R.W. thought.

He slipped into his room and dressed in civilian clothes, jeans he'd worn before getting drafted. They were three sizes too big.

"Where are you going?" Mom called when she heard him open the front door.

"I'm gonna take the car to town. I'll be back in an hour."

He closed the door before she could respond.

### 

At Mel's Tavern, they wouldn't take R.W.'s money. Any God-fearing son of Ronald Wilkens who served his country could drink three-two beer on the house.

R.W. wasn't going to argue. In many states he was too young to legally drink, and definitely too young to vote. If they wanted to roll out the red carpet here, let them.

But nothing was free. He soon tired of repeating how his dad had died, of telling them what they wanted to hear about Vietnam, how if the politicians would let them, the troops could wipe out the whole country in one solid week. And being asked what he thought of those long-haired sissies over there on the campus. Man, if Ronald Sr. were still alive and fit, he'd know what to do with them.

After several beers, R.W. made his escape. They hardly noticed, they were so busy repeating stories about World War II and arguing with one another over who did what. He walked toward the campus. The closer he got, the more students he saw. Hippies, kids his age and older, wearing their strange garb, but no stranger than many of the GIs in Nam.

This was the first time he'd seen real dyed-in-the-wool protestors. They were a small, scattered group, carrying signs, joking with one another and laughing.

These were the Commies that were ruining our campuses and trying to overthrow the government? he asked himself.

They were kids, his age. They were raised in the same country as he, some in the same town and neighborhood, by the same kind of parents, in the same kind of houses. They couldn't be Communists. Communists were the NVA, gooks who came at you in the night, who hid in holes and haunted your dreams in your bed.

He had to go home. Even his crying mother was better than this.

### ###

Monday night they went to Erma's play. R.W. napped, slept off most of the alcohol, but had a hangover pounding his head. As his mother requested, he wore his dress greens.

He couldn't believe how well Erma could sing—sounded just like Joni Mitchell.

They waited for Erma to come from backstage.

"You did wonderfully," Mom said.

"It was great, sis."

With his arm around Erma's waist and Mom's shoulders, they followed the crowd out the gymnasium doors. The man in front of them looked over his shoulder. He was oriental, and R.W. tried to ignore him.

"Hey soldier-boy, you just get home?" He was in his forties, long-haired and tall.

"Yes, I did."

"You been in Vietnam?"

R.W. nodded. The man turned all the way around and flipped a ribbon on R. W.'s uniform jacket. "Did you have to kill any children to get those?"

They'd stopped walking, parting the milling crowd who

swarmed around them.

"Get out of my way, mister."

"You kill babies over there? Women, too?"

Before R.W. could think, he took a half-step forward, spun the man around, wrapped an arm around his throat, and put him on the floor.

Erma grabbed R.W.'s arm, the only thing restraining him from punching the guy's face. "I could kill you. But I won't. Not in front of my family." Erma's crying had gotten through to R.W.

The man crawled away backwards. "You're crazy. They're making you guys crazy over there. They're sending back monsters."

R.W. straightened. "You're the monster."

He took Mom and Erma by the arms and led them outside.

### 

The funeral was on Tuesday. They played taps, then lowered Dad in the ground with a twenty-one gun salute. They presented Mom with the stars and stripes.

The vets from Dad's VFW post shook R.W.'s hand and told him how sorry they were. R.W. thanked them all for attending. Many were coming to the house afterwards. R.W. knew it would be a long day.

### 

It was almost May. R.W. called the army and asked for an extension of leave, since his dad had died. He needed the extra time to help put his mother's house in order before he returned to Nam.

He also requested stateside duty. Both requests were taken under consideration to be given an answer in twenty-four hours.

He went through Dad's old army pictures, putting them in an album for mom. "Dad's insurance from the mill will more than cover the funeral expenses. Mom, will you live off what's left?" R.W. asked.

Mom got up on a chair to fix the top of the drapes. She refused to answer the question. Feeling frustrated, R.W. simply rubbed his hands on his forhead. He knew this was not the time to ask these questions.

R.W. told his mom, "I'm going to go outside and work on the yard. I'll fix those pictures later. Better yet, why don't you have Erma do that when she gets home from school?"

The next two days were R.W.'s happiest since coming home. He mowed, painted the eaves, turned over the soil in Mom's flower beds, and trimmed the hedge.

On the second evening, he put a new rope on the swing and Erma took off her shoes and stood in the tire while he pushed.

When it was his turn, he told her to stand back and made the swing go as high as the rope would allow.

It was reckless, but he closed his eyes and felt the pleasant spring breeze on his sweaty face. Why couldn't he fly, be as carefree as this felt, as he used to when he spent hours and hours out there swinging high while Dad mowed the yard. Home had protected him then. Its walls—his father. But that was all over now. All over.

"You're going to break your neck," Erma called, funneling her voice through cupped hands.

When he finally slowed the swing, she grabbed the rope as soon as she could. "What's with you R. W.?"

He jumped off the tire. "Why?"

"You're different. What happened over there? Is it really like they say? Have you killed people?" Erma asked in a soft voice.

"That's all it boils down to, isn't it?" yelled R.W. "How many have you killed—for you, for the press, for the guys at Dad's bar!"

"Dad's bar, R.W.? What's with all this drinking?"

"I have a few drinks, so what?"

"You never did before. I can see a beer now and then, but you're sneaking hard stuff."

"I'm not sneaking. I just don't want Mom to get upset."

Erma laughed. "If Mom found the bottle sitting in the middle of your bed, she'd swear it was cologne. You don't have to worry about Mom."

She sounded so much older, he was speechless.

"And I hear you in there at night rolling around in your sleep, moaning and groaning. What's going on with you, R.W.? Was that guy right at the school? Are they . . . turning you into monsters over there?"

She couldn't have wounded him more deeply if she'd shot him through the heart. He was suddenly afraid, afraid he was horribly abnormal and couldn't see it.

"Do I seem like a monster?" he asked her casually, desperately needing to hear the answer.

She plunked down on the swing. "No . . . not a monster. But you seem . . . troubled."

The confusion hit again. *This didn't mean nothing.* Did it? Yes, it did. It was here, in his real life. The "nothing" part was in Nam. Except for Doc and Stone."

"R.W. did you . . . kill anybody?"

He felt sick, and suddenly fearful. But there was nothing to be afraid of, so why was his heart racing? "Sometimes in war you have to kill, Erma."

"What was it like? Was it like they say, our guys shooting women and children?"

*But . . . it didn't mean nothing.* That was the thing she could never understand, so it was hopeless to explain. If he told her it didn't mean nothing, she'd run away shrieking. Or ask him what the hell he was talking about. Because here . . . everything mattered.

Absolutely everything.

###

May 1st, the Army answered R.W.'s requests. They would give him a twenty-day extension; however, he would have to return to Vietnam. A plane ticket was enclosed.

Erma's high school graduation was five days before he had to report to Oakland, California, on the 20th. With all the trouble going on at Kent, she asked him if he would take her there to fill out some papers for college next year. She was accepted and had paid her tuition, but needed to apply for scholarship funds for the second semester now that Dad wouldn't be around to pay the bills.

R.W. had avoided the campus since that first Sunday. The last couple of weeks he'd avoided everything, sitting in Dad's chair, watching Walter Cronkite give the evening news about Vietnam, spending hours in his room, sitting on the glider in the backyard, keeping himself just the other side of sober.

"Why don't you look up some of your old friends?" Erma had asked him.

But he had no old friends he ever wanted to see again. The past only reminded him of who he used to be. He found that very confusing and depressing.

If he could fulfill Erma's request, maybe he could leave here feeling better about himself. Besides, a lot was happening on that campus. He didn't want her to go there alone.

May 2nd, on Saturday morning the local radio news reported that there was trouble on the campus again. Some students held a dance in the middle of North Water Street. When an irate driver gunned his motor, students swarmed all over his car, smashing his windows and conducting other acts of violence, or as some put it, terrorism. The mayor set a curfew and had the bars emptied, and the students were herded back to the campus by 11:00 p.m.

The next morning, R.W. accompanied Erma to the college. There were a lot of people milling about—white students, hippies, and blacks, but things seemed more festive than threatening.

They could forget getting into the Administration building. Whites and blacks were jamming the place, seeking permission for a rally that night on campus.

"We'll try again Monday," R.W. told Erma.

Sunday morning, he listened to the local report while Mom and Erma went to church. All hell had broken loose at Kent on Saturday night. The students had held their rally with permission, but the group of eight hundred had gotten out of hand, eventually setting fire to the ROTC building. The mayor had called in five hundred National Guardsmen and declared a state of emergency. Later the students went on to stage a sit-down strike in the middle of a busy intersection, and four hundred more Guardsmen were called in.

Sounded like a war zone to R.W. No way he'd let Erma go there alone.

###

Monday afternoon, May 4th, was bright and sunny. R.W. noticed how fatigued the National Guardsmen looked, like he and Stone that first night after guard duty at the LP zone. Mac told them they'd get used to it, and they did.

Students crossed the campus holding their books, a sign to R.W. that it was back to business as usual, he thought. He grabbed Erma's arm and jumped when someone started to gong the heavy campus bell.

"Relax, R.W.," Erma laughed, "it's just a bell."

About a thousand students were gathering on the ground called the Commons. A crowd twice that size was watching on the periphery.

"Nothing bad can happen with so many people. There aren't enough cells in the world to lock this many up," Erma reasoned. "Let's just watch for a couple of minutes."

Against R.W.'s better judgment, they joined the ring of onlookers. Two students came by and handed them pamphlets—some rhetoric about the campus being theirs and no one having the right to tell them differently. R.W. gave his pamphlet to Erma.

Officers drove across the campus in jeeps speaking through

bullhorns: "Evacuate the Commons area. Evacuate the Commons area. This assembly is unlawful. Go home. You have no right to assemble." A rock or two bounced off the jeep.

"Pigs off campus!" students hollered back. "One-two-three-four, we don't want your fucking war."

The Guardsmen cracked open their M79s and put something inside. R.W. hoped it was only gas.

They fired in the direction of the crowd. A couple of the students retrieved a canister or two and tossed them back. The students cheered, but when the gas broke up the crowd, several Guardsmen gave chase. The whole Commons area was a haze of gas. R.W. grabbed Erma's arm and pulled her farther up the hill where the air was still clear.

This was the other side of the war, and it was happening right here, in his own hometown. Kids were ripping off their shirts, covering their mouths and noses.

"We've got to leave, Erma."

R.W. was sweating profusely.

"No," she yanked her arm away. "I'm not going. This is wrong, and I won't leave them. The war is wrong, and these guards are wrong, and the curfew is wrong. I won't leave."

R.W. cursed under his breath. "Then you do exactly what I tell you." He led Erma, careful to keep an eye out for places he could shelter her if they fired those M1s.

Over the next hour, the mood of the crowd changed. Some of the students were angry, throwing stones at the guards, yelling obscenities.

It was only a matter of time before the two sides clashed and blood was spilled. Something bad was about to happen, but R.W. was as engrossed as Erma in the drama. These protestors were serious. They didn't want the war. And surprisingly, something rose up inside of him, too. He didn't want it either.

Yet he stayed on the periphery. He wasn't sure that what they were doing was right. Why didn't they protest at an army base? Why here?

Almost immediately, he knew the answer. Because this was where they lived. This was their world—their sanctuary. And it was also his.

They were saying they mattered—that their lives had meaning— that they had a right to be heard, to say, "No, I'm not going. You can't have me, my body, my soul, my life. I don't believe in what you're doing. I won't go. I won't bless you with my blood."

When he heard the shots, R.W. pulled Erma to the ground, lying half on top of her.

"What's happening?" she screamed.

R.W. waited until it was over. At first glance, he could see at least two down. It looked like a man and a woman. The Guardsmen had fired into the crowd. He couldn't believe it. They fired into the crowd. His own were killing his own.

### ###

Hours later, Erma was still in her room. She didn't come out to eat supper, but lay in there crying. His mother had rattled on about the Communists taking over the campus, but when Erma and R.W. had lost patience with her, she'd withdrawn into her knitting and hadn't spoken since.

There wasn't a great deal of Vietnam coverage on the national news. It was mostly about operation Fishhook, Nixon's newest effort, going into Cambodia and flushing out the North Vietnamese strongholds.

*That's where I'm supposed to be,* R.W. thought to himself. He wondered about Stone and Doc and the new troops—Even and the rest. He should be there; they needed him. War was people, not a military action. Not a government action. It was only people.

Today was May 4th. Since they crossed the International Dateline to go to Nam, it was May 5th over there. He knew their guys were involved in the Fishhook. What were they doing right now? Would they believe what he'd witnessed today?

### ###

The following morning, local news coverage announced that four students had been killed by the National Guard during the Kent State incident, and nine others were wounded. They weren't able to identify who'd started it.

R.W. kept listening to the sentiments. He got a haircut. Everywhere it was the same, even from the old guys he'd listened to all his life. "What's it really like over there? If we had a crack at them, we'd wrap it up in two weeks. Give us two weeks, and we'd have the bastards on the run."

If it wasn't for Doc and Stone, he wouldn't go back. He wanted to be finished with Vietnam and a country that shot down its own.

### 

May 18th, the day after his sister's graduation, R.W. knocked on Erma's door. She bade him come in. Her room was still decorated in pink and white. Sitting in the middle of her canopy bed writing out thank you cards, she looked like a princess.

Her gaze went to the letter he carried in his hand.

"Did that come today?"

"Yeah."

"Who's it from?"

R.W. sat on the bed. "It's from Doc, my friend." A rush of tears made
R.W. fight hard to compose himself. He had to swallow the grief before he could finish.

"On May the 5th, same day those students got wasted, my unit went into Cambodia to bring out POWs. They didn't get there in time, figured they'd missed the evacuation by less than an hour. On the way out, they were ambushed and took a lot of losses. A guy I rode over with on the plane, name of Stone, was one of the ones . . . killed. Doc told me not to come back. We had the charm, us three. I think I broke it when I came home. I got Stone killed."

R.W. broke down, crying. Slumping forward, putting his elbows on his knees, hands to his forehead, shoulders shaking, he was quiet at first, then gasping and sobbing from deep down. Erma rushed to softly close her door so Mom wouldn't hear.

"R.W., you've been drinking. I can smell it all over this room. You've got to get a hold of yourself. I'm so sorry about those men, but you can't blame yourself."

She didn't understand. How could he possibly explain? All at once, he realized how truly alone he was, how locked into the periphery of Nam, with no way out. She couldn't know how frightening it was, to know your life wasn't shit.

He felt her small hand patting his shoulder. She was scared. The sooner he took his troubles away from this house, the better for her and mom.

Erma shoved a wad of tissues in R.W.'s hand, and he wiped his face. "I killed Stone. That's just the way it is."

"R.W . . ."

He cut her off, "I talked to some of the protestors today, a couple of vets out of Nam. There's a place in Canada called Sanctuary. I'm gonna head there tomorrow."

Erma sank down to the powder-blue carpet, her quilted robe puddling around her knees. "It's gonna break Mom's heart."

"I have to go. They'll throw my ass in jail for desertion. I've got no more choice now than when I was drafted. Doc got out, but if I go back to Nam, I'll die for sure. Maybe I deserve that after what I did to Stone, but I can't be a part of Vietnam anymore. God's gonna have to kill me someplace else."

"Don't say that R.W. How can you say that? I don't want you to go."

R.W. put his arms around Erma. He knew her innocence; she was so young and sweet, so clean. He kissed her forehead. "You take care of yourself, sis. Take care of mom. I'll always tell you where I'm at, but you gotta promise to keep it to yourself."

"Okay, Ronnie."

"I'm gonna write to Mom. When you guys get up in the morning, I'll be gone."

"Here." She padded across the carpet to her dresser, opened her silver jewelry box and took out some bills. "You take this. I insist."

He counted fourteen dollars. "I don't need your money." He held it toward her, but she pushed his hand away.

"You might not need it now, but you could later. Take it."

After another tearful hug, R.W. went back to his room, and found pen and paper.

*Dear Mom,*

*I want you to know I love you, but it's time for me to go. I don't want you to be sad, I don't need that, and I don't want you to worry. I watched those kids die on the parking lot. I'm still fighting, Mom, the war is my responsibility, and I've got to fight the only way I see fit.*

*Love, R.W.*

He folded the letter, laid it on the kitchen table, gathered his few belongings, and walked out the house. At the end of the street, he looked back only once, saw the swing, and knew he could never return.

# LONG BEN, VIETNAM, 1970
# CHAP STONE
# CHAPTER 15

> "God knows how to get a man's attention."
>
> —Chap Stone

On May 10th, a nurse walked to the hospital bed in Long Ben, South Vietnam. The young man she'd been taking care of had been unconscious for over a week. He suffered from a major concussion, shrapnel wounds in the right leg, and had yet to speak a word. Other than that, his body was basically whole.

There was a story going around about him, that he was the luckiest man in South Vietnam. He'd been wearing his flack jacket when hit, a move which had saved his life. The two pieces of shrapnel had been stopped at his right breast, only puncturing the skin and muscle, not able to enter the chest cavity.

Now if he'd regain consciousness, the story might be true.

The nurse bathed him for the second time this week and had just wrung the water from the sponge when she noticed him looking at her.

*Angels are for the afterlife,* Chap thought to himself. *Am I dead?*

He knew he had eyes, because he could see her. He had ears because he heard her call, "Sergeant? Sergeant can you hear me?"

He wiggled his feet.

"Do I have legs?" His throat was sore.

"You're all right, Sergeant. You're in the hospital. You're fine."

When he moved his legs, they were so sore he groaned.

His right shoulder was so tender, he couldn't move it. When he wiggled his fingers, she told him to be careful of the sutures.

"Where am I at?"

"You're at Long Ben hospital, Medivac unit. They're getting ready to take you back stateside."

"What happened to the guys who were with me?"

The nurse didn't answer.

"What happened to the people that were with me?"

She didn't answer.

The third time, he tried to rise. "Please, tell me what happened to the people that were with me."

The nurse had heard only rumors. They weren't good. "I don't know all of it. Most of the guys that were with you are dead. I'm sorry."

"Who made it and who didn't?"

She said, "I don't know that."

"Doc . . . Roger . . ."

She pushed against his shoulders. "I don't know."

Stone figured there weren't many left. He knew they'd walked into an ambush. Fate intervened with him.

"Ellie? Is Ellie here?"

"I don't know any Ellie. Now rest."

He thought of Doc, but the haze from medication kept him from getting a tight hold on Doc's fate. He was probably dead. Doc. Dead.

Lucky R.W. wasn't there. He shouldn't try to come back.

Stone's thoughts drifted. He couldn't sleep yet; he had to think. There were five thousand dollar wounds on his shoulder and head. He was alive. Slowly and quietly he said a prayer asking where Doc was.

"God . . . oh God . . ." It would have to be enough, this prayer. It would have to be enough because he had no more words. Vietnam had taken all of his prayers. But what he couldn't speak aloud, he had written in those small books, like Top had told him to. When he was better, he would write it all down, every word of it. He would never let them go—Hood, Ernson, Top, Ellie, R.W., French Fry, Neil, Hattie. Doc. He would never let them go, and the world would know they'd been here and what they'd given.

There was no greater love. None greater than laying it down. Every day. Laying it down scared. Laying it down with rage. Laying it down with duty. No greater love.

The nurse bent over him. She smelled sweet, like the new hay back home in Neosho. "You're the luckiest man in Vietnam," she said.

"I am?"

He didn't hear answer. He fell asleep.

**THE END**